O ‖‖‖‖‖‖‖‖‖‖ N

Wine Country

GUIDEBOOK

Lisa —!
Enjoy...
Cindy

"Where there's wine,
there's joy."
– Socrates

2009 EDITION

Oregon Wine Country Guidebook
First Edition
Copyright ©2009 Half-Full Enterprises

ISBN: 978-0-9791201-2-1

Printing by Journal Graphics; Portland, Oregon

Oregon Wine Country is exploding with new wineries and
vineyards entering the scene literally every two weeks!
Things will change here and there, but every effort has been
made to maintain accuracy. However, Half-Full Enterprises
cannot fully guarantee that the information in this book is
or will be accurate and cannot accept responsibility for any
complications that may arise from using the information in
this book. Finally, you are responsible for your own actions,
before, during and after using the information provided in
this book. Drink responsibly! Half-Full Enterprises is not liable
for any irresponsible actions on your part, including but
not limited to taking a wrong turn on a trip, tripping, buying
excessive quantities of wine, drunk dialing, hooking up with
an ex-boyfriend or girlfriend, or hurting yourself, your car, or
someone else. Be smart.

<u>Cover Photos</u> (clockwise from top left)

Mt. Hood View – Photo by Cindy Anderson
Balanced Wine – www.istock.com © Kristine Buharinska
Harris Bridge – Photo by Cindy Anderson
Van Duzer Field – © 2009 Christina Weber, photographer
Territorial's Wine Bar – Photo by Cindy Anderson

Half-Full Enterprises
10350 N. Vancouver Way; Suite 173
Portland, OR 97217
www.winecountryguidebook.com
email: cindy@winecountryguidebook.com

Acknowledgements

Dedication

This book is dedicated to my father, Brad Anderson, who passed away just before this book went to print. He really was the World's Greatest #1 Dad and is loved and missed.

Thank you, thank you, thank you!

Huge thanks to my partner in love and wine, Steve Woods. Great job taking photos! Thanks for coming along to enjoy all the rides (and for driving too). It's been a wonderful journey up and down the long and winding roads of Wine Country – and life! Cheers to many, many more...

Also, big cheers go out to Helene Wren for her very helpful contributions and enthusiasm to chip in with interviews, write-ups and photos. You're the best!

I was thrilled with all of Christina Weber's author bio photos. Thanks, Chrissy! (www.christinaweber.com).

A special thank you to Ed Querfeld for his photographs too.

Kudos to Mary Beth Saddoris for her eagle eyes in editing. I highly recommend her! (writebrainediting@gmail.com)

Thanks as well to all my hard-working friends who helped me "research": Christy Langan, Del Profit, Naira Perez, Heidi Randall, Ed and Angela Querfeld, Suzanne Richardson, Kurt and Sherrie Martel, Mona Das (and Blake), Kelly Martin and Krista McCracken, Luis Chaname and Judi Jamison, and Chrys Pappas. And to all the "Top Ten List" contributors: We *all* thank you for passing along your knowledge.

Apologies to any vineyards I missed. Be cute and be open.

"Sorrow can be alleviated by good sleep, a bath, and a glass of good wine."

– *St. Thomas Aquinas*

Discoveries

As you can imagine, researching Oregon's Wine Country was a blast! I was a big fan before writing this book, but still discovered lots of surprises:

The Passion!
Meeting winemakers and hearing them proudly rave about their wine always put a smile on my face. They are deeply committed specialists who truly do it for love – and it shows.

Wine Festivals
Sure, it's always fun to go and imbibe, but it's also a rare opportunity to taste different brands of wines side-by-side. You'll get to learn what you really like. Take advantage!

Few and Not Far Between
Instead of trying to run around to 5-6 wineries, just pick a few to savor and enjoy. Focus on a limited geographic area and give yourself some time-outs to sit and sip.

Take Notes
It *seems* like you'll remember particular wines, but it's a good idea to write down the ones that are stand-out favorites. You're tasting for a reason. Space is provided on each page of this book so you can take note of the most appealing samples. Wine Shop Sommeliers can look at these top picks and make educated guesses and recommendations for your specific palate too.

A Day in the Country
What a great mini-vacation! An afternoon in Wine Country is a very relaxing break that can take you away from the everyday. It really is a great escape!

Concerts
Many places have concert nights throughout the summer. Ask around at your favorite places. Vineyards make for a great envionment to see live music!

Contents

Wineries (Note color-coded bars at top of page)

Willamette Valley North

Willamette Valley South

Southern Oregon

Other Oregon

Maps/Color Key

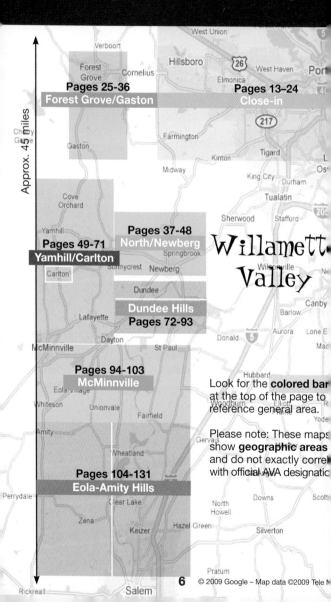

Approx. 45 miles

West Union

Verboort

Hillsboro · 26 · West Haven · Port

Forest Grove · Cornelius · Elmonica

Pages 25-36
Forest Grove/Gaston

Pages 13–24
Close-in

217

Cherry Grove

Gaston

Farmington

Kinton · Tigard

Midway

King City · Durham

Cove Orchard

Yamhill

Pages 49-71
Yamhill/Carlton

Carlton

Sunnycrest · Springbrook

Newberg

Pages 37-48
North/Newberg

Willamette Valley

Tualatin

Sherwood · Stafford

Wilsonville

Dundee

Dundee Hills
Pages 72-93

Lafayette

Dayton

McMinnville · St Paul

Barlow

Aurora · Lone E

Donald

Canby

Mac

Pages 94-103
McMinnville

Eola Village

Whiteson · Unionvale

Amity

Fairfield

Wheatland

Pages 104-131
Eola-Amity Hills

Perrydale

Zena

Clear Lake

Keizer

Hazel Green

Hubbard

Look for the **colored bar** at the top of the page to reference general area.

Please note: These maps show **geographic areas** and do not exactly correl with official AVA designatic

Yode

Gervais

North Howell

Downs

Silverton

Scott

Rickreall

Salem

Pratum

6

Maps/Color Key

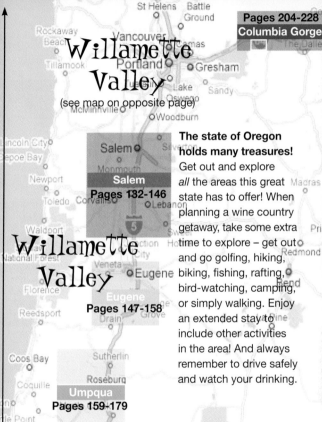

St Helens · Battle Ground

Pages 204-228
Columbia Gorge

Rockaway Beach · Vancouver · Camas · The Dalles

Willamette Valley

Tillamook · Portland · Gresham · Lake Oswego · Sandy

(see map on opposite page)

McMinnville · Woodburn

Lincoln City · Depoe Bay

Salem · Silverton

Monmouth

Salem
Pages 182-146

Newport · Madras

Toledo · Corvallis · Lebanon

Waldport · Junction City · Sweet Home · Prineville

National Forest · Veneta · Redmond

Florence · Eugene · Bend

Eugene
Pages 147-158

Reedsport · Cottage Grove · Drain

Coos Bay · Sutherlin

Coquille · Roseburg

Umpqua
Pages 159-179

Myrtle Point · Canyonville

Port Orford

Southern Oregon

Joaquin · Eagle Point

Grants Pass

Gold Beach · Cave Junction · Medford · Klamath Falls

Rogue Valley
Pages 180-203

Brookings · Ashland

Crescent

The state of Oregon holds many treasures! Get out and explore *all* the areas this great state has to offer! When planning a wine country getaway, take some extra time to explore – get out and go golfing, hiking, biking, fishing, rafting, bird-watching, camping, or simply walking. Enjoy an extended stay to include other activities in the area! And always remember to drive safely and watch your drinking.

© 2009 Google – Map data ©2009 Tele Maps

How to Use this Book

Colored bar at top of page indicates designated map areas. Note that these are not entirely grouped by AVA, but rather by convenient *geographic areas* for mapping.

**Red triangle =
on-site vineyard**

**Brown triangle =
tasting room**

A word about:

Hours: Information is current at the time of this printing, but subject to change. CALL if you need a confirmed open time, as websites are often out of date. You can usually make an appointment to taste on a weekday or in off-season months. When you see (Mem-Thanks) listed, it means Memorial Day weekend through Thanksgiving weekend. Wine Season and summer are loosely mid-May through Labor Day or mid-Oct. Most everything is closed on major holidays; *maybe* including the Superbowl, Easter and July 4th.

Tasting Fee: This fee is typicaly WAIVED with purchase! Inquire about the exact requirements for refund.

Wine: Here, you will get an idea of how many different kinds of wine a winery will typically carry (understanding that wine seasons change, and things sell out). Price range excludes high-end reserve wines. And of course, wineries "specialize" in *every* wine they make, but I called out one or two highlights.

Map Symbols

●   Indicates on-site vineyard

●   Dot-only means vineyard(s) located elsewhere

About Maps

Wine Country really is out in the *country*, and full of winding farm roads that change names every few miles, are not marked well (or at all), get washed out, or are gravel. It's truly best to prepare – and pack your patience! Some areas are clearer than others with more blue road signs to direct you, but it's always worth extra planning. And don't let getting lost deter you from exploring. Enjoy the ride and the beautiful passing scenery!

Maps in this book
I've tried to mark only the roads you'll need to know about to find the area wineries. Be aware that there is not a lot of detail, as this would almost double the book's handy size.

Suggestions:

- Pick your first winery and download directions from their website. Bigger wineries are generally easier to find and often have blue directional signs off the highway, so they might be the best place to start your day. Once you are there, you can ask for good directions to the next place, and so on. Pay attention and make sure you truly understand where they are sending you. Have your co-pilot listen too!

- Ask for directions as soon as you know something is awry. Gas stations often have younger staff, so you may need to find a helpful customer or look at a map after getting your bearings.

- GPS navigators, including Mapquest and Google Maps, may attempt to take you on some pretty crazy "short-cuts". Double reference things if possible, especially when there are a lot of roads involved. Cell phone coverage can be spotty between hills and valleys, but try calling your target winery to help guide you in.

 Highway 99 (aka N. Pacific Hwy.) runs along much of Oregon's Wine Country and is typically quite near the interstate, Hwy. 5. Look for this wine-colored road on maps to get your bearings. Other important highways are indicated in **black.**

Icons

A picture is worth a thousand words!
Here's an explanation of what they mean...

■ A solid wine-colored icon is the equivalent of an "A" – like you got in school. It means they are solid in this area.

■ A screened back wine-colored icon is like a B or C – it means pretty good, but not 100% there for some reason.

■ A gray icon means not-so-much, n/a or no.

view

Solid camera icon means it's a great place to take pictures and enjoy the extra-stunning view!

Lighter pink camera icon means you might not be able to see the view from the tasting room, or that it's nice, but won't *quite* take your breath away, or you have to walk a bit to see the view.

Gray camera icon means no view to speak of.

fanciness

Solid glass icon means they had a big budget to work with and made things especially nice. Reserved for places that appear impressive.

Lighter pink icon is the basic, average place. Most fall into this category. Nice, but not too nice.

Gray glass icon means it's extra casual here (and little attempt at any stylish decor).

deck/patio

Solid patio icon means there is a great place to sit outside on an extra nice deck or patio with view.

Lighter pink patio icon means it's pretty good, but maybe not stellar. Sometimes there are not enough tables, or they are just little wood picnic tables, or there is no real view.

Gray patio icon means no outside seating.

Icons

ood for sale

Solid food icon means you can buy food here!

Lighter pink food icon means you can buy nibbles or light snacks, possibly restricted to summer months or weekends only. Phone first.

Gray food icon means no food available.

picnic area

Solid picnic icon means you'll get plenty of space to lay out your picnic blanket (as opposed to al fresco lunching on a deck or patio). A solid icon means you'll get a great view too!

Lighter pink picnic icon means there will be some space to picnic on a flat area, but the view might not be totally spectacular.

Gray picnic icon means no space to picnic.

bus/rv

Solid bus icon means a big bus or RV has plenty of room to drive in – and turn around.

Lighter pink bus icon means it's not easy. Call.

Gray bus icon means don't bring a big bus.

pet friendly

Solid dog icon means dogs are welcome! Might need to use a leash, but there's some room to run.

Lighter pink dog icon means use leash.

Gray dog icon means dog must stay in the car.

tours

Solid tour guide icon means RSVP for tour. Easy!

Lighter pink tour guide icon means maybe...

Gray tour icon means they do not give tours.

event space

Solid party icon means good place for events. Call winery directly for more info on rentals.

Lighter pink party icon means call for details.

Gray party icon means you cannot host here.

You *must* RSVP for large groups and tours!

Wineries absolutely need you to call ahead for any group larger than 6-8 people, and don't assume that your limo company will do it for you. Be aware that some wineries will charge a small fee for groups, which may or may not include a tour, private tasting, or food. Be sure to ask!

Taking a guided tour of a winery can be fun – RSVP ahead of time and learn a little about the wine-making process.

Plan ahead

Pick about 3-4 wineries and don't try to do too much. Slow down and enjoy! Be sure to take time out for a picnic and some porch-sitting. Maybe even take a little walk. Or lay out a blanket for a nap! Fill up your gas tank and bring water.

Designate a driver

Be really careful about your drinking. There are lots of limos, buses and shuttles around, so take advantage of these services and save a ticket or a life! Consider dumping or spitting. You can share tastes as a way to try more wines and drink less.

Keep your patience

It's pretty common and easy to get a bit lost here and there. Keep your cool and ask for directions. Relax!

Closed holidays

It's a given that wineries will be closed on major holidays (Christmas Eve, Christmas Day, and New Years Day). It's a good idea to call to inquire about other holidays like Easter, 4th of July, and Christmas week. Memorial Day and Thanksgiving weekends are party times!

Do NOT bring wine from another winery

I can't believe anyone would ever do this, but apparently they do. Rude. Don't even think about it. When having lunch at a winery, you obviously must have their wine.

Portland Area

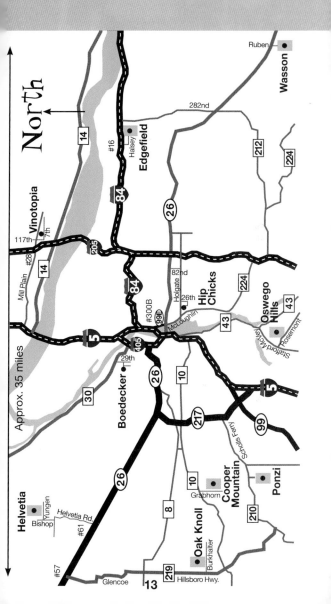

decor

food for sale

event space

gift shop

Boedecker
• •

www.boedeckercellars.com
2621 NW 30th Avenue; Portland; 503.288.7752

Hours: Fri 2:00pm–7:00pm; Sat–Sun 1:00pm-5:00pm
(year-round)

Tasting Fee: $5.00 for 5 tastes

Wine: 12 varieties; $13.00–$45.00
Specializes in Pinot Noir

Notes: An urban winery close to Portland's "Trendy-Third"/Nob Hill restaurant and shopping neighborhood.
• Contemporary, artsy space in old, huge warehouse with room to host events big or small. • The owners, Stewart and Athena, are a well-blended married couple that have divergent preferences when it comes to making wine. To solve this problem, they split lots into "Stewart" and "Athena" bottlings. The results are fun to try – small-production, food-oriented, distinctive Pinot Noir and Chardonnay from some of Oregon's greatest vineyards. • "The Portland Wine Project" building also hosts Grochau Cellars or gc. Contact them directly for tasting appointment (503.224.5778).

Facts: Established 2003 • Uses sourced grapes all throughout Oregon • 3,000 cases annually

Owners: Stewart Boedecker and Athena Pappas
Winemakers: Stewart Boedecker and Athena Pappas

Date visited: _____
Went with: _____
Notes: _____

Cooper Mountain

www.coopermountainwine.com
9480 SW Grabhorn Road; Beaverton; 503-649-0027

Hours: Daily 12:00pm-5:00pm year-round

Tasting Fee: $8.00 for 5 tastes

Wine: 10 varieties; $15.00–$50.00
Specializes in Organic, Biodynamic Wines

Outside: Located just minutes from Portland, this winery is situated within a residential neighborhood. The coastal range provides a great view when sitting on the grass or at a picnic table.

Inside: The quaint tasting room features warm, yellow and orange walls and a wood tasting bar. The walls are filled with educational information about the vineyard and organic, biodynamic faming.

Notes: Founder, Dr. Robert Gross' winery features many of his own personal standards of alternative farming and wine making practices. First U.S. winery to gain the label approval for a no-sulfite added wine.
• Friendly with parties on summer Wednesday nights.
.

Facts: Established 1987 • 110 Acres • Willamette Valley AVA • 16,500 cases annually

Owner: Dr. Robert J. Gross
Winemaker: Giles De Doming

Date visited: _____
Went with: _____
Notes: _____
_____

view

fanciness

deck/patio

food for sale

picnic area

bus/rv

pet friendly

tours

event space

Edgefield Winery

www.mcmenamins.com/edgefield
2126 S.W. Halsey; Troutdale; 503.665.2992

Hours: Fri–Sat 12:00pm–10:00pm;
Sun–Thurs 12:00pm–9:00pm (year-round)

Tasting Fee: $3.00 for 5 "classics" tastes;
$5.00 for 5 tastes (choice of 3 different flights)

Wine: 20 varieties; $13.00–$24.00
Specializing in variety

Outside: Come for a taste, stay for a weekend! This totally unique, 74-acre property has a historic hotel, winery, brewery, *and* distillery, fine dining, several pubs, beer garden, movie theater, golf, and a spa!

Inside: Low ceilings in a true wine cellar (basement) with big windows to see tanks and barrels. True to style, whimsical art adorns walls and what-not.

Notes: Check their website for hotels in wine country including the Grand Lodge in Forest Grove, the Hotel Oregon in McMinnville, Kennedy School in Portland, and a new downtown Portland hotel coming early 2010

Facts: Established 1990 • 3 producing on-site acres (sources from 13-15 vineyards throughout OR and WA) • Willamette Valley AVA • 21,000 cases

Founders: Brothers Mike and Brian McMenamin
Winemaker: Davis Palmer

Date visited: _____
Went with: _____
Notes: _____

Helvetia Winery

www.helvetiawinery.com
23269 Yungen Road; Hillsboro; 503-647-5169

Hours: Fri-Sun 12:00pm-5:00pm Summer;
Sat-Sun 12:00pm-5:00pm Winter

Tasting Fee: $2.00 for 4-7 tastes

Wine: 7 varieties; $11.00–$32.00
Specializing in Pinot Noir and Chardonnay

Outside: A taste of country life! The red, 100 year-old farm house is surrounded by lots of nature, so make sure to give yourself time to sit out on the deck and watch for passing wildlife.

Inside: Farmhouse is home to their tasting room and information center. The walls are filled with old photos and history of the winery and of the area of Helvetia.

Notes: Swiss/German historic farmhouse with year-round Christmas tree farm. • During the summer, tribal fisherman sell smoked salmon. • Custom labels!

Facts: Established 1970 • 13 acres • Willamette Valley AVA • 13,000 cases annually

Founders: James Platt and Former Congresswomen Elizabeth Furse
Winemaker: James Platt

Date visited: _____
Went with: _____
Notes: _____
_____

decor

food for sale

event space

gift shop

Hip Chicks Do Wine

www.hipchicksdowine.com
4510 SE 23rd Ave; Portland; 503.234.3790

Hours: Daily 1:00pm-6:00pm (year-round)

Tasting Fee: $5.00 for 6+ tastes; $5.00 for Tiernan Conner flight; $8.00 for both

Wine: 15 varieties; $14.00-$24.00
Specializes in making fun wine and wine fun

Notes: Follow the directional sandwich boards when driving through the large industrial park to find this urban winery. • Inside, you'll sip among the barrels and all. It's a bit shy on hip, chic decor. • Don't miss the "Drop Dead Red" (she is full of mysterious intrigue that cannot be ignored) or the infamous "Belly-Button wine! • Be sure to get on their newsletter list – these girls know how to have fun. Check website for parties

Facts: Established 2001 • Uses grapes from vineyard all throughout OR and WA • 5,000 cases

Owners: Wine Goddess, Laurie Lewis and the Wine Maven, Renee Neely
Winemakers: Laurie Lewis and Renee Neely

Newberg Tasting Room
602B East First Street, Newberg; 503.554.5800
Hours: Daily 12:00pm–7:00pm

Date visited: _____
Went with: _____
Notes: _____
_____

ew

iness

/patio

or sale

c area

s/rv

iendly

urs

space

Oak Knoll

www.oakknollwinery.com
29700 SE Burkhalter Road; Hillsboro; 800.625.5665

Hours: Daily 11:00am-5:00pm (year-round)

Tasting Fee: $5.00 for 6 tastes

Wine: 10 varieties; $10.00–$34.00
Specializing in Pinot Gris and Fruit Wines

Outside: Beautiful rolling hills and a large lawn space used for summer concerts surround the tasting room. The tasting room, while modern on the inside, has a rustic-chic, unfinished look to the outside.

Inside: Large, fun and energetic tasting room. Hand-painted grape vines on the warm yellow walls and a resident kitty both give charm to the easy going atmosphere. Gifts too.

Notes: Named for its surroundings, and the area's abundance of oak trees. • Bocce, croquet, volleyball and badminton! • Large lawn area for picnics and many summer concerts! • Oldest winery in Washington County.

Facts: Established 1970 • Sources grapes from throughout Oregon • 35,000 cases annually

Founders: Ron and Marj Vuylsteke
Winemaker: Jess Herinckx

Date visited: _____
Went with: _____
Notes: _____

view

fanciness

deck/patio

food for sale

picnic area

bus/rv

pet friendly

tours

event space

Oswego Hills

• •

www.oswegohills.com
450 South Rosemont Road; West Linn; 503.655.2599

Hours: Sunday 12:00pm-5:00pm (year-round)

Tasting Fee: FREE for 6+ tastes

Wine: 12 varieties; $15.00–$25.00
Specializing in traditional methods (let grapes guide)

Outside: Who would guess that just minutes from
the city sits this peaceful array of truly *pretty* barns?
Fresh, bright and white, it's like a little farm village
right from the pages of Disneyland – but for adults.

Inside: Open-air, open room, with freshly-painted
white bead board floor-to-ceiling. Clean and neat with
two tasting tables and a Roy Rogers cut-out for fun.

Notes: Take the left turn just past Lake Oswego Public
Golf Course. • Originally homesteaded as an Arabian
horse stable in the early 1940s. Roy Rogers kept
horses here! • Good wine, Moonstruck chocolate and
other nibbles served with a smile by friendly folks.

Facts: Established 2001 • 15 acres planted (since
1997, plus sources from Columbia Valley) • Willamette
Valley AVA • 3,000 cases annually

Owner: Jerry Marshall
Winemaker: Derek Lawrence

Date visited: _____
Went with: _____
Notes: _____
_____

Ponzi

●●●●●●●●●●●●●●●●●●●●●●●●●●●

www.ponziwines.com
14665 SW Winery Lane; Beaverton; 503.628.1227

Hours: Daily 10:00am-5:00pm (year-round);
Until 8:00pm Friday and Saturday nights in summer

Tasting Fee: $10.00 for 3-5 tastes

Wine: 12 varieties; $17.00–$60.00
Specializing in creating a variety of wines

Outside: Absolutely beautiful vines and woods surround the vineyard. Big, well-kept lawn is a perfect spot to relax or enjoy a picnic.

Inside: Large tasting room with Northwest touches. Tends to be busy and can be hard to get personal attention.

Notes: Dick Ponzi is a local legend, being one of the very first pioneers to bring Pinot to Oregon. • Named "Oregon Winery of the Year 2009" Wine Press NW • Live music Sundays 6:00pm-9:00pm all summer. • Don't miss **Ponzi Wine Bar** (503.554.1500) or **The Bistro** (503.554.1650) both at 100 SW 7th in Dundee.

Facts: Established 1970 • 120 Acres • Chehalem Valley AVA • 30,000 cases annually

Owners: Dick and Nancy Ponzi
Winemaker: Loisa Ponzi

Date visited: _____
Went with: _____
Notes: _____
_____

view

fanciness

deck/patio

food for sale

picnic area

bus/rv

pet friendly

tours

event space

St. Josef's

• •

www.stjosefswinery.com
28836 S. Barlow Road; Canby; 503.651.3190

Hours: Sat–Sun 11:00am-5:00pm (year-round);
Mon–Fri 11:00am–5:00pm (summers – best to call)

Tasting Fee: $5.00 flight of 6+ tastes

Wine: 12 varieties; $9.00-$24.00
Specializes in Pinot Noir and Pinot Gris

Outside: A quick, half-hour drive from Portland takes
you worlds away to this old-style German hideaway
with a fountain entry courtyard and on-site small lake.

Inside: Manor-like touches with massive wooden
entry doors, a giant staircase and dark golden walls.

Notes: St. Josef Winery, named after the founding
father, has a history going back more than 25 years,
being family-owned and operated with three generations involved. And even before that, Josef's grandfather had a winery in Central Hungary. • The nearby
town of Aurora has lots of antique stores. • St. Josef's
is not plotted on the "Close-in" map. See their website.

Facts: Established 1983 • 64 acres (42 producing)
• Eastern Willamette Valley AVA • 10,000 cases

Owners: Josef and Lilli Fleischmann and family
Winemaker: Josef Fleischmann

Date visited: _____
Went with: _____
Notes: _____
_____

cor

or sale

space

shop

Wasson Brothers
• •

www.wassonwine.com
17020 Ruben Lane; Sandy; 503.668.3124

Hours: Mon-Sat 9:00am-5:00pm;
Sun 11:00am-5:00pm (year-round)

Tasting Fee: FREE for 4 tastes

Wine: 18 varieties; $6.00–16.00
Specializing in specialty fruit and berry wines

Notes: Former farmers, these identical twin brothers
started the winery together with their love of fruit and
wine in mind. • Conveniently located in downtown
Sandy, only minutes outside of Portland, this working
winery with tasting room is an easy stop on your way
to Mt. Hood. • There are many wine gifts, along with
tools and ingredients for personal home wine making
and home beer brewing. • The oldest winery in
Clackamas County, featuring many fruit wines from
all local fruit. • Feel free to ask for a tour.

Facts: Established 1981 • 7 acres • East Willamette
Valley AVA along with other grapes sourced from
throughout the state • 4000 cases annually

Owners: Twin brothers Jim and John Wasson
Winemaker: Jim Wasson

Date visited: _____
Went with: _____
Notes: _____
_____

decor

food for sale

event space

gift shop

Vinotopia
· ·

11700 Se 7th Street; Vancouver, WA; 360.213.2800
www.cinetopiatheaters.com

Hours: Daily 11:30am-10:30pm (year-round)

Tasting Fee: Varies $1.00–$10.00
You'll buy a computerized card that allows you
to select tastes from over 75 preserved wines

Wine: 75+ varieties; $13.00–$45.00
Specializes in sampling a huge variety of Oregon,
Northwest and other wines

Notes: And now for something totally different! This
unique tasting room is located inside Vancouver's
"Cinetopia" state-of-the-art movie theater. The Wine
Bar and Restaurant, Vinotopia, hosts a myriad of
carefully selected Northwest wines, as well as others
from around the globe. You'll be absolutely astounded
by the beautiful array of wine! Taste brands and/or
varietal styles side-by-side and find your favorites.
Have dinner at the stylish, open restaurant near the
stunning fireplace. Or weather permitting, relax in
the serene outdoor garden patio space surrounded
by flowers and fountains. • Wine classes offered first
Tuesdays of each month with registration. • Check
calendar for live music in dining room. • They have
an officially great Happy Hour! 3:00pm-6:00pm and
8:00pm-10:00pm with $5.00 wine and $4.00 appetizers.

Date visited: _____
Went with: _____
Notes: _____
_____

Forest Grove/Gaston

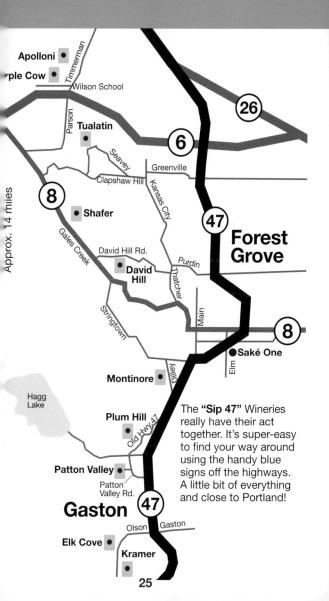

Apolloni

rple Cow

Timmerman

Wilson School

Parson

Tualatin

Seavey

Greenville

6

26

Clapshaw Hill

Kansas City

8

Approx. 14 miles

Shafer

Gales Creek

David Hill Rd.

David Hill

Purdin

Thatcher

47

Forest Grove

Stringtown

Main

8

Dilley

Montinore

Elm

Saké One

Hagg Lake

Plum Hill

Old Hwy 47

The **"Sip 47"** Wineries really have their act together. It's super-easy to find your way around using the handy blue signs off the highways. A little bit of everything and close to Portland!

Patton Valley

Patton Valley Rd.

Gaston

47

Olson   Gaston

Elk Cove

Kramer

25

view

fanciness

deck/patio

food for sale

picnic area

bus/rv

pet friendly

tours

event space

Apolloni

••••••••••••••••••••••••••••••••

www.apolloni.com
14135 NW Timmerman; Forest Grove; 503.330.5946

Hours: Fri–Sun 12:00pm–5:00pm (year-round)

Tasting Fee: $5.00 flight of 6–7 tastes

Wine: 10–12 varieties; $13.00–$30.00
Specializes in Pinot Noir and Italian-style wines

Outside: A quick trip up a country road leads you to the big, white barn with aluminum siding (sorry, it's *not* that gorgeous mansion high on the hill). The vines and trees here are close-in rather than way out. Nice rock garden back patio.

Inside: Very basic interior with cement floors and corrugated tin walls. Taste the wine right next to the barrels the wines are fermenting in (bring a sweater).

Notes: Unique, Italian-style wines. • Apolloni is the namesake of owner's family, who has been making wine in Italy for 300 years (Alfredo grew up spending summers in Italian vineyards, helping and learning).

Facts: Established 2002 • 40 acres • North Willamette Valley AVA • 3,500 cases annually

Owners: Alfredo and Laurine Apolloni
Winemakers: Alfredo Apolloni and Anne Hubatch

Date visited: _____

Went with: _____

Notes: _____

_____

David Hill

• •

www.davidhillwinery.com
46350 NW David Hill Road; Forest Grove; 503.992.8545

Hours: Daily 12:00pm–5:00pm (year-round)

Tasting Fee: FREE flight of 6+ tastes

Wine: 18 varieties; $10.00–$30.00
Specializes in Pinot Noir and Port

Outside: The whole farm area, and in particular the refurbished historic farmhouse, is entirely Americana sweetness at its finest. An obviously wonderful place for an outdoor picnic with its big front (or is that back) yard and lots of white picnic tables.

Inside: Yesteryear charm and simple style. Two light-filled rooms with a small gift shop, fireplace and bar.

Notes: Originally homesteaded in 1883, complete with grapes (torn out during prohibition in 1913).
• This historic home with tasting room is located on David Hill on David Hill Road (named way back in the day, as was another of David's namesakes: Hillsboro).

Facts: Established 1992 • 140 acres (40 planted in 1965) • North Willamette Valley AVA • 9,000 cases

Owners: Milan and Jean Stoyanov
Winemaker: Jason Bull

Date visited: _____
Went with: _____
Notes: _____
_____

view

fanciness

deck/patio

food for sale

picnic area

bus/rv

pet friendly

tours

event space

Elk Cove
• •

www.elkcove.com
27751 NW Olson Road; Gaston; 503.985.7760

Hours: Daily 10:00am–5:00pm (year-round)

Tasting Fees: $5.00 flight of 5-7 tastes

Wine: 12 varieties; $19.00–$48.00
Specializes in Pinot Noir, Pinot Gris and Pinot Blanc

Outside: Stunning, expansive views in all directions and partially nestled in a cove surrounded by lush hills. Lots of outdoor deck and picnic seating with a big wooden gazebo down in the small valley. Pretty!

Inside: Giant windows line the circular tasting room so you can enjoy the outside while sipping inside at the big, three-sided bar. Northwest upscale-rustic with natural woods and a teepeed skylight ceiling.

Notes: One of Oregon's oldest wineries. • Many award winning wines at this family-owned and operated vineyard. • Big elk head presides over the bar! • Wine Press Northwest 2007 Pacific NW Winery of the Year.

Facts: Established 1974 • 600 acres with 200+ under vine (four separate sites in the Northern Willamette Valley) • 35,000 cases annually

Owners: Pat, Joe and Adam Campbell
Winemaker: Adam Godlee Campbell

Date visited: _____
Went with: _____
Notes: _____

Kramer

●●●●●●●●●●●●●●●●●●●●●●●●

www.kramerwine.com
26830 NW Olson Road; Gaston; 503.662.4545

Hours: Daily 12:00pm–5:00pm (Apr–Oct.);
Thurs-Sun 12:00pm–5:00pm (Nov–Mar)

Tasting Fees: Free (Basic 6+); $5.00 Premium (4-5)

Wine: 18 varieties; $10.00–$40.00
Specializes in big variety; Sparkling and Pinot Noir

Outside: Country-rustic, super-friendly, small, casual.
Rolling hills everywhere with views from the small porch
or patio. Out back and down the path, there's a second
party area for picnics, parties and weddings.

Inside: Smallish room and bar with big gift shop and
small-town, country charm-and-style.

Notes: The friendly and fun staff here have genuine
enthusiasm for the wine county experience. • Tasty
palette cleansers are provided and you can get a
good cup of coffee too. • LIVE certified. • They *love*
their doggies here, and even dedicate labels to them.

Facts: Established 1989 • 20 acres • Yamhill-Carlton
AVA •1,500 cases annually

Owners: Trudy and Keith Kramer
Winemakers: Jon Armstrong and Anne Hubatch

Date visited: _____
Went with: _____
Notes: _____
_____

view

fanciness

deck/patio

food for sale

picnic area

bus/rv

pet friendly

tours

event space

Montinore Estate
● ●

www.montinore.com
3663 SW Dilley Road; Forest Grove; 503.359.5012

Hours: Daily 11:00am–5:00pm (year-round)

Tasting Fee: $5.00 flight of 5 tastes

Wine: 15–18 varieties; $13.00-$32.00
Specializes in wide range of 100% estate wines

Outside: Upon driving through the Montinore gates, you'll notice why they call this an estate. The grandeur sets in at the entrance and goes all throughout, and all maintained with warmth and ease.

Inside: Everything is BIG here: it's a big room with a big bar and big windows. Although it's very fancy, it retains a nice friendliness. Tasting room is in the winery facility (not in the cool historic home next door).

Notes: Strict, biodynamic and sustainable practices (certified). • Live music on Sunday afternoons through out the year. • Homesteaded in 1905 by a man who thought it looked just like his home in Montana, so he named it "Mont-in-Ore" or Montana in Oregon.

Facts: Established 1982 • 230 acres (producing)
• North Willamette Valley AVA • 36,000 cases annually

Owner: Rudy Marchesi
Winemaker: John Lundy

Date visited: _____
Went with: _____
Notes: _____
_____

Patton Valley

• •

www.pattonvalley.com
9449 Old Hwy 47; Gaston; 503.985.3445

Hours: Thur–Sun 11:00am–5:00pm (Mar–Nov)

Tasting Fee: $5.00 basic flight of 3-4 tastes;
$5.00 premium taste

Wine: 6 varieties; $20.00-$70.00
Specializes in Pinot Noir

Outside: The most spectacular sights will hit you
on the exit drive back down the road, so keep your
eyes peeled for the incredible view laid out before you!
They are gifted with a great view, but not set up for it.

Inside: The focus really is on the wine here, and so as
not to distract you, there's little attention paid to decor.
You'll taste right next to the cool storage room (nice
way to beat the summer heat).

Notes: LIVE certified and incredibly dedicated to
sustainable methods. • Cherry Hill is the parent
company of Patton Valley Vineyard.

Facts: Established 2000 (1997 plantings) • 72 acres
(24 planted) • North Willamette Valley AVA • 3,000
cases annually

Owners: Monte Pitt and Dave Chen
Winemakers: Monte Pitt and Jerry Murray

Date visited: _____
Went with: _____
Notes: _____
_____

view

fanciness

deck/patio

food for sale

picnic area

bus/rv

pet friendly

tours

event space

Plum Hill

• •

www.plumhillwine.com
6505 SW Old Highway 47; Gaston; 503.781.4966

Hours: Mon–Sat 11:00am–5:00pm;
Sunday 12:00pm–5:00pm (year-round)

Tasting Fee: FREE flight of 5 tastes

Wine: 6 varieties; $12.00-$24.00
Specializes in Pinots

Outside: This cute little ranch home adds country
appeal to surrounding hillsides with views of Mount
St. Helens and Mt. Adams. Ample picnic space,
covered deck/patio. Live music on summer Sundays

Inside: Fresh, sweet and brand-new tasting room
with big windows for big views. It's part cozy living
room (complete with fireplace), part gift shop with
local art, and part tasting bar.

Notes: Fun fountain o' wine at the entrance. • They
give their vines a personality, creatively calling them
names like General Cluster, Albert Vinestein, or The
Grapeful Dead. • Picnic food and sandwiches for sale

Facts: Established 2008 • 35 acres • North Willamette
Valley AVA • 200 cases annually

Founders: RJ and Juanita Lint
Winemaker: RJ Lint

Date visited: _____
Went with: _____
Notes: _____
_____

Purple Cow

• •

www.purplecowvineyards.com
52720 NW Wilson School; Forest Grove; 503.756.0801

Hours: Saturday only 11:00am–5:00pm (year-round)

Tasting Fee: $5.00 flight of 5 tastes

Wine: 8 varieties; $12.00-$32.00
Specializes in experimenting (i.e. Tempranillo)

Outside: This small Oregon working farm/vineyard
is a relaxing setting for the very friendly tasting room
located in the owner's ranch home. Summertime is
the best time, when you can sit outside and enjoy the
views from the porch, benches or party area!

Inside: You'll feel right at home here where you taste
in the living room. A whole new place is in the works.

Notes: Their wine varietals are all named after women
(i.e. daughters). • The name *Purple Cow* comes from
a small, plastic purple cow toy which the Armstrong's
daughter played with.

Facts: Established 2005 • 8 acres • North Willamette
Valley AVA • 700 cases annually

Owner: Jon Armstrong
Winemakers: Jon Armstrong and Anne Hubatch

Date visited: _____
Went with: _____
Notes: _____
_____

decor

food for sale

event space

gift shop

Saké One

• •

www.sakeone.com
820 Elm Street; Forest Grove; 1-800-550-SAKE

Hours: Daily 11:00am-5:00pm (year-round)

Tasting Fee: $3.00 for 4 tastes; Optional reserve and specialty flights available

Wine: 18+ varieties; $11.00-$39.00
Specializing in handcrafted saké

Notes: Discover the secrets of saké! The only sakéry in Oregon and the only U.S.-owned saké brewery in the country. • Right off Hwy. 47 for an in-town, urban experience. Not super Zen, but super fun! •. The on-site saké brewery has a painted mural on the building depicting the process and history of saké brewing. • Lots of gifts, ranging from teas, chocolates, and artesian saké servingware available for purchase, with knowledgeable staff that wants to share information and their love of sake. • Summer concert series (see website). • Free daily tours are a must, as they are a great way to see the full process of how saké is made and a chance to explore the behind-the-scenes process. • Sulfite-free. • No need to bow or take off your shoes. Smile and say SOCK-ay!

Facts: Established 1997
Sakémaster: Greg Lorenz

Date visited: _____
Went with: _____
Notes: _____
_____

ew

ness

patio

or sale

c area

s/rv

iendly

urs

space

Shafer

●●●●●●●●●●●●●●●●●●●●●●●●●●●●

www.shafervineyardcellars.com
6200 NW Gales Creek Road; Forest Grove; 503.357.6604

Hours: Thurs–Mon 11:00am–5:00pm (year-round)

Tasting Fee: FREE flight of 6+ tastes

Wine: 24 varieties; $10.00-$38.00
Specializes in Riesling and Sparklings

Outside: Take a nice Sunday drive up through the
farm, totally off the beaten path. Picnic food is available here, so take a moment to slow down and have
a seat on the front porch or in the gazebo.

Inside: Ho, ho, ho! It's Christmas 365/24/7 here! The
huge Christmas shop here sits merrily within the winery
and tasting room. Rustic, country-crafty charm.

Notes: Inviting and super-friendly. You can tell they
love what they do and enjoy welcoming all guests,
neighbors, friends and visitors alike. • Cheese and
crackers, coffee and even chocolate are typically
offered.

Facts: Established 1978 • 70 acres (40 planted)
• North Willamette Valley AVA • 12,000 cases annually

Owners: Harvey and Miki Shafer
Winemakers: Harvey and Miki Shafer

Date visited: _____
Went with: _____
Notes: _____
_____

view

fanciness

deck/patio

food for sale

picnic area

bus/rv

pet friendly

tours

event space

Tualatin Estate
• •

www.tualatinestate.com
10850 NW Seavey Road; Forest Grove; 503.357.5005

Hours: Sat–Sun 12:00pm–5:00pm (closed Jan–Feb)

Tasting Fee: FREE flight of 6+ tastes

Wine: 10–12 varieties; $10.00-$40.00
Specializes in Burgundian varietals

Outside: Nestled in the hills and surrounded by rows upon rows of old vines. Expansive views in every direction and a big area for picnicing under the trees with lots of tables provided – or bring a blanket!

Inside: Simply styled tasting room with natural wood floors, ceiling, back bar, tables and tasting bar. Nice big windows give you a view while sipping.

Notes: Tualatin's motto is "Old vines. New vision." They go *way* back. • Check the website for occasional summer concerts. • Owned by "sister winery" Willamette Valley Vineyards (they share grapes). • LIVE and Salmon-Safe certified.

Facts: Established 1973 • 200 acres (40 planted) • North Willamette Valley AVA • 12,000 cases annually

Owner: Jim Bernau
Winemaker: Forest Klaffke

Date visited: _____
Went with: _____
Notes: _____
_____

North/Newberg

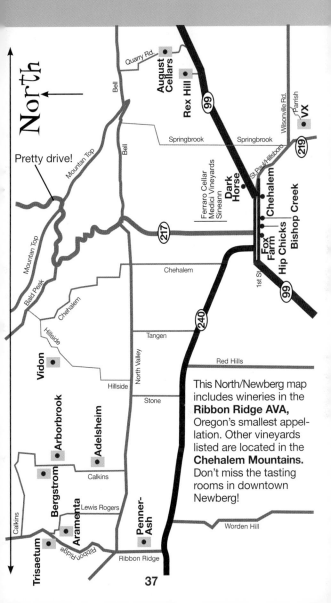

North

Pretty drive!

Quarry Rd.

August Cellars

Rex Hill

99

Wilsonville Rd.

Parrish

VX

219

Bell

Springbrook

Springbrook

Mountain Top

Bell

Ferraro Cellar
Medici Vineyards
Sineann

Dark Horse

St. Paul/Hillsboro

Chehalem

Bishop Creek

217

Chehalem

Fox Farm

Hip Chicks

1st St

99

Chehalem

Mountain Top

Bald Peak

Hillside

Tangen

240

North Valley

Red Hills

Vidon

Hillside

Stone

Arborbrook

Adelsheim

This North/Newberg map
includes wineries in the
Ribbon Ridge AVA,
Oregon's smallest appel-
lation. Other vineyards
listed are located in the
Chehalem Mountains.
Don't miss the tasting
rooms in downtown
Newberg!

Bergstrom

Calkins

Lewis Rogers

Aramenta

Penner-Ash

Worden Hill

Trisaetum

Calkins

Ribbon Ridge

Ribbon Ridge

view

fanciness

deck/patio

food for sale

picnic area

bus/rv

pet friendly

tours

event space

Adelsheim

• •

www.adelsheim.com
16800 NE Calkins Lane; Newberg; 503.538.3652

Hours: Wed-Sun 11:00am-4:00pm (year-round)

Tasting Fee: $15.00 for 4-5 tastes

Wine: 15 varieties; $19.00–$68.00
Specializing in Pinot Noir

Outside: This unique building perched on the edge
of the vineyard features a tower much like a light-
house looking out onto the grapes. Their back patio
is a perfect spot for a picnic lunch where you'll be
surrounded by fantasic views of the Chehalem Valley.

Inside: Gorgeously remodeled tasting room! Huge,
curved, stone-and-wood tasting bar equipped with
a plentiful and pleasant tasting room staff. Even on
a busy day you will get personal attention!

Notes: Ginny Adelsheim is the artist behind all the
wine labels, each featuring a different strong woman
who is important to the Adelsheim family. • Practices
sustainable farming techniques.

Facts: Established 1971 • 180 acres • Willamette
Valley and Chehalem AVAs • 50,000 cases annually

Owners: David and Ginny Adelsheim
Winemaker: David Paige

Date visited: _____
Went with: _____
Notes: _____
_____

Aramenta

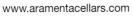

www.aramentacellars.com
17979 NE Lewis Rogers Road; Newberg; 503.538.7230

Hours: Daily 10:30am–5:00pm (year-round)

Tasting Fee: $10.00 flight of 5 tastes

Wine: 3 varieties; $20.00–$48.00
Specializes in Pinot Noir and Claret

Outside: Nice! The area outside the tasting room is tropically landscaped. A small fountain and patio at the entrance, with two cozy deck areas overlooking the vineyard, a small pond, and the hills beyond.

Inside: A big, rust-colored wooden barn with raw wood walls opening to the storage room (bring a sweater). There's very little window action, so you'll want to hang outside to enjoy the gorgeous view.

Notes: Previously a long-established fruit and nut orchard, first vines were planted in July 2000 • Named after the great-great-grandmother, Ethel Aramenta Evans-Carter, who farmed the property organically long before it was chic. • 100% out-the-door sales.

Facts: Established 2003 • 28 acres • Ribbon Ridge AVA (Oregon's smallest AVA) • 1,000 cases

Owners: Ed and Darlene Looney
Winemakers: Ed and Darlene Looney

Date visited: _____
Went with: _____
Notes: _____
_____

view

fanciness

deck/patio

food for sale

picnic area

bus/rv

pet friendly

tours

event space

ArborBrook

• •

www.arborbrookwines.com
17770 NE Calkins Lane; Newberg; 503.538.0959

Hours: Thur–Fri 11:00am-3:00pm and Sat–Sun 11:00am-5:00pm (year-round)

Tasting Fee: $10.00 for 3-4 tastes

Wine: 4 varieties; $18.00–$60.00
Specializing in Pinot Noir

Outside: Charming, rustic, red barn gives this tasting room a sense of country fun. Surrounded by vines and views of the Chehalem Valley, this delightful vineyard has an entirely pleasant, down-to-earth feel.

Inside: Newly-renovated 1910 vintage barn with a nice balance of old and new. Modern tasting room with the authentic charm of the original barn. Once a hazelnut sorting room, the tasting room is now a place to sip wine and talk with either Mary or Dave, who strive to keep the family feel in their winery.

Notes: Named after the old willow tree and creek on the property. • Very friendly and approachable.

Facts: Established 2004 • 11 Acres • Chehalem Valley AVA (plus other vineyards) • 2,000 cases

Owners: Dave and Mary Hansen
Winemaker: Laurent Montalieu

Date visited: _____
Went with: _____
Notes: _____
_____

cor

for sale

space

shop

August Cellars

• •

www.augustcellars.com
14000 Ne Quarry Road; Newberg; 503.554.6766

Hours: Daily 11:00am–5:00pm (May–Oct); Fri–Sun
11:00am–5:00pm (Nov–Apr)

Tasting Fee: FREE Flight of 6–7 tastings;
$5.00 fee each for groups of 6 or more

Wine: 13 August Cellars varieties; $10.00-$30.00;
11 or more from tenants $18.00–$40.00

Notes: Industrial, winery-mod in style, this very cool
and contemporary building makes cement, iron and
rivets look beautiful. The 16,000 sq.ft. facility was
built with great attention to decor, smart design and
the environment. Outside, picnic under the giant firs.

Facts: Established 2002 (public tasting room 2004)
• 42 acres in Chehalem AVA, and uses sourced grapes
from throughout all of Oregon • 3,500 cases annually

Owners: The Clarence Schaad Family
Winemaker: Jim Schaad

Artisanal Wine Cellars • Tom and Patricia Feller
Barking Frog Winery • Ron Helbig
Crowley Wines • Tyson Crowley
Et Fille • Jessica Mozelco
Toluca Lane • Jeffery and Lane Crowther
Laura Volkman Vineyard • Laura Volkman

Date visited: _____

Went with: _____

Notes: _____

_____

Bergström

view

fanciness

deck/patio

food for sale

picnic area

bus/rv

pet friendly

tours

event space

Bergström

• •

www.bergstromwines.com
18215 NE Calkins Lane; Newberg; 503.554.0468

Hours: Daily 10:00am-4:00pm (year-round)

Tasting Fee: $20.00 for 5-7 tastes

Wine: 12 varieties; $20.00-$65.00
Specializes in Pinot Noir and Chardonnay

Outside: Gorgeousness surrounds the grape vines, with views of Mt. Jefferson and the Chehalem Valley. This winery has an extra-fantastic deck, so plan extra time to unwind, relax, kick back and enjoy!

Inside: Tuscan-style touches and beautiful wood and granite wine bar give this intimate tasting room an elegant flair. Be sure to look in all directions.

Notes: Try the Epicurean Experience, a private food and vintage wine pairing for you and five guests (see website). • The name and label is from the Bergström family seal. • All wines are organic. • Upcoming second label: "ö." • Estate wines are organic and biodynamic.

Facts: Established 1999 • 40 acres • Dundee Hills AVA (plus sources throughout OR) • 10,000 cases

Owners: John and Karen Bergström; Josh and Caroline Bergström
Winemaker: Joshua Bergström

Date visited: _____
Went with: _____
Notes: _____
_____

ew

iness

/patio

for sale

c area

s/rv

riendly

urs

t space

Penner-Ash

●●●●●●●●●●●●●●●●●●●●●●●●●●●

www.pennerash.com
15771 NE Ribbon Ridge Road; Newberg; 503.554.5545

Hours: Wed-Sun 11:00am-5:00pm (Feb-Dec)

Tasting Fee: $5.00 for 4-6 tastes; Specialty flights sometimes available, such as their Pinot Noir flight

Wine: 12+ varieties; $10.00–$65.00
Specializes in Pinot Noir

Outside: Luxurious, romantic, and beautiful with views from every angle of the Coastal Range, Chehalem Valley, Mt. Hood and Mt. Jefferson. Bring a picnic lunch, relax, and enjoy the scenery!

Inside: Modern, natural woods with clean lines and a rotating art gallery. The entire working winery can be viewed through big windows to witness fall crush.

Notes: Unique winemaking style. • Private tours and barrel tastings available by appointment. • Winery tours Saturdays 10:00am and Sundays 11:00am (RSVP). • A romantic, perfect place to bring a date!

Facts: Established 2005 • Willamette Valley AVA • 80 acres on-site (plus sources from select Oregon vineyards) • 10,000 cases annually

Owners: Rob and Lynn Penner-Ash
Winemaker: Lynn Penner-Ash

Date visited: _____
Went with: _____
Notes: _____
_____

view

fanciness

deck/patio

food for sale

picnic area

bus/rv

pet friendly

tours

event space

Rex Hill

● ●

www.rexhill.com
30835 NW Hwy 99W; Newberg; 800.739.4455

Hours: Daily 10:00am–5:00pm (wine season);
Daily 11:00am-5:00pm (winter)

Tasting Fee: $10.00 flight of 5-6 tastes

Wine: 15 varieties; 3 brands; $25.00-$52.00
Specializes in Pinot Noir, Pinot Gris, and Chardonnay

Outside: This large, gray winery was once a fruit
and nut processing plant built in the 1930s. Terraced
garden with covered picnic areas, giant abstract
sculpture and a view up the vineyard-covered ridge.

Inside: The beautifully carved door sets a fancier
tone for the interior. The vaulted ceilings, red terra
cotta floors and fireplace surround a large bar area.

Notes: Look into Rex Hill's wine education classes
(check out the info at www.pinotnoir.com). • Don't
forget to draw a pig in the guest book (no peeking)!

Facts: Established 1995 • 373 acres • Dundee Hills
AVA • 10,000 cases annually

Owner: Paul Hart (A-Z WineWorks owns Rex Hill)
Winemakers: Cheryl Hanson, Sam Tannahill, Cheryl
Francis, Michael Davis
William Hatcher Label: Bill Hatcher

Date visited: _____
Went with: _____
Notes: _____
_____

Trisaetum
• •

www.trisaetum.com
18401 Ribbon Ridge Road; Newberg; 503.538.9898

Hours: Thur-Sun 11:00am-4:00pm (May-Sep);
other times by appointment

Tasting Fee: $10.00 for 5 tastes; Extra $5.00 for tour

Wine: 7 varieties; $28.00–$85.00
Specializing in Pinot Noir and Riesling

Outside: Very romantic! The state-of-the-art, brand new winery has a clean modern look to it, both outside and inside the building. Ex-hazelnut ranch.

Inside: Art gallery showcases owner James Frey's original art work, all inspired from the vineyard. A tour of this winery is a must, not only to see where the wine is made but more importantly to view the incredible "barrel cave" where all the barrels are stored.

Notes: Winery named after owners children, Tristen and Tatum. • Everyone from the owners to the wine tasting attendants helps with fall crush—making this truly a unique, artisan winery • All wines are organic.

Facts: Established 2005 • 50 acres • Ribbon Ridge and Yamhill/Carlton AVA • 1,000 cases annually

Owners: James and Andrea Frey
Winemakers: Greg McClellan and James Frey

Date visited: _____
Went with: _____
Notes: _____
_____

view

fanciness

deck/patio

food for sale

picnic area

bus/rv

pet friendly

tours

event space

VX (Vercingetorix)

www.vxvineyard.com
8000 NE Parrish Road; Newberg, OR; 503.538.9895

Hours: Sat–Sun 12:00pm–5:00pm (Mem–Thanks)

Tasting Fee: $1.00 per taste

Wine: 5-6 varieties; $16.00–$28.00
Specializes in Pinot Noir

Outside: Smack-dab in the middle of the countryside, all just a couple miles from downtown Newberg. This 200-acre farm also hosts Willamette Valley Farms hazelnut orchard with snacks, coffee and oils for sale. Nice wooden deck for a picnic lunch or party.

Inside: Simple and open triple-garage barn with hand-painted mural of wine country and barrel bar.

Notes: Pronounced VERsin-GETa-riX. • Named after the Gallic hero with clan that fought against Roman invasions and Caesar's army with a scorched earth strategy that spared nothing except the beloved vineyards of Burgundy (home of Pinot Noir). • Good place for a long walk on their tree-shaded drive.

Facts: Established 2003 • 8 acres (producing) 200 acres total • Willamette Valley AVA • 1,500 cases

Owners: Willamette Farms LLC / The Hall family
Winemaker: Jason Silva

Date visited: _____
Went with: _____
Notes: _____
_____

Vidon

• •

www.vidonvineyard.com
17425 NE Hillside Drive; Newberg; 503.538.4092

Hours: Sat–Sun 12:00pm–5:00pm (year-round);
plus by appointment

Tasting Fee: $10.00 for 6+ tastes

Wine: 9 varieties; $18.00–$39.00
Specializes in Pinot Noir

Outside: Pretty, wide-open spaces surround this barn-style tasting room and winery. Sit outside under the big tent or at one of the front tables for some sun.

Inside: Recently upgraded bar area with stained concrete floors and natural wood pretty much everywhere.

Notes: LIVE, Sustainable and Salmon-Safe certified.
• The name VIDON (vee-DOAN) comes from the owners' names, "Vicki" and "Don." • The bee symbol on the labels comes from an old, well-house on the property that contained a very large hive between its studs (bees were *everywhere* and and many stories and adventures followed)!

Facts: Established 2004 • 20 acres • Chehalem Mountains AVA • 700-900 cases

Owners: Vicki and Don Hagge
Winemaker: Don Hagge

Date visited: _____
Went with: _____
Notes: _____
_____

Area Tasting Rooms

Bishop Creek
www.bishopcreekcellars.com
614 E. First Street; Newberg; 503.487.6934
Hours: Wed–Sun 1:00pm–7:00pm
Tasting Fee: $8.00 for 4 tastes; $10.00 with special pour
Wine: 5 varieties; $18.00–$28.00
Urban-rustic style with brick walls and First Friday parties.

Chehalem
www.chehalemwines.com
106 South Center Street; Newberg; 503.538.4700
Hours: Thurs–Mon 11:00am–5:00pm
Tasting Fee: $5.00 core flight (3); $10.00 reserve flight (3)
Wine: 16 varieties; $19.00–$44.00
Cool and artsy with bright colors (but known for their whites).

Dark Horse/Medici (Medici Vineyards, Sineann Wines and Ferraro Cellar)
www.ferrarocellar.com; www.sineann.com
1505 Portland Road; Newberg; 503-538-2427
Hours: Daily 11:00am–5:00pm (May-Nov);
Fri-Mon 11:00am–5:00pm (Dec-April)
Tasting Fee: $5.00 for 8-10 tastes
Wine: $16.00–$42.00
Traditional style with back porch. All wines made at Medici.
Sineann at Medici Vineyards Saturdays 11:00am–5:00pm.

Fox Farm Wine Bar
www.foxfarmvineyards.com
602A E. First Street; Newberg; 503.538.VINO
Hours: Daily 12:00pm–close (wine bar hours!)
Tasting Fee: $4.00 for 4 tastes
Wine: 11 varieties; $16.00–$36.00
Traditional style with brick; wine bar with snacks and beer.

Hip Chicks Do Wine
www.hipchicksdowine.com
602B E. First Street; Newberg; 503.554.5800
Hours: Daily 12:00pm–7:00pm
Tasting Fee: $7.00 for 6 tastes
Wine: 15 varieties; $14.00–$24.00
Cool, loft-style, almost coffee-shoppy kind of place.

Yamhill-Carlton

Yamhill

Willakenzie

Lenné

Moores Vly Rd.

Main St

Laughlin

Yamhill-Newburg Hwy

North Valley

Ribbon Ridge

47

240

Carlton
Winemakers
Studio

Laurel
Ridge

Kuehne

Cana's
Feast

Hendricks

Oak Springs Farm

Abbey Rd.

Main Street

Carlo
& Julian

**Downtown
Carlton Map**
see page 57

Mineral Springs

Anne
Amie

Abbey Rd.

47

McMinnville

99

99

Further on south down the "Sip 47" path and surrounding the town of Carlton are several wineries with varied, unique styles. The tasting rooms of downtown Carlton are plotted on their own map and in their own section (which follows this one). Note that the Dundee Hills are nearby in the area due east.

view

fanciness

deck/patio

food for sale

picnic area

bus/rv

pet friendly

tours

event space

Anne Amie

• •

www.anneamie.com
6580 NE Mineral Springs; Carlton; 503.864.2991

Hours: Daily 10:00am–5:00pm (Apr–Nov);
Fri–Sun 10:00am–5:00pm (Dec–Mar)

Tasting Fee: $5.00 4–5 tastes; $10.00 premium
flight; $10.00 Port and chocolate pairings

Wine: 12 varieties; $17.00–$35.00
Specializes in cool climate whites

Outside: Spectacular, high hilltop view with vistas
of vineyards, valleys and the Pacific Coast Range.
Beautifully landscaped and well-manicured grounds
.

Inside: Elegant, old-country Tuscan-manor-style with
welcoming charm, white marble bar, and a long "living
room." French doors line the full back wall and lead
to an expansive, stately terrace and stellar view!

Notes: LIVE certified vineyards • Tours at 11:00am
for $30.00 including reserve tasting and Pinot Noir
glass. • Named after Ann and Amy, Pamplin's two
daughters and "amie" also means "friend" in French

Facts: Established 1999 • 150 acres • Yamhill-
Carlton AVA • 12,500 cases annually

Owner: Dr. Robert Pamplin
Winemaker: Thomas Houseman

Date visited: _____
Went with: _____
Notes: _____
_____

Cana's Feast

www.canasfeastwinery.com
750 W Lincoln Street; Carlton; 503.852.0002

Hours: Daily 11:00am–5:00pm (year-round)

Tasting Fee: $5.00 flight of 5 tastes

Wine: 13 varieties with three labels (Bricco, Cana's Feast, Cuneo); Specializes in Italian varietals, Burgundy, Bordeaux, and Rhône-style red wines

Outside: Stunning Tuscan-style winery and tasting room plus restaurant located right off Hwy. 47 with hillside views of the coastal range. Two exceptional deck areas. Test your bocce ball skills on two courts.

Inside: The tasting room is tastefully done in an Italian winery theme with vaulted ceilings and arched doorways. Friday night dinner and weekend lunch served in the charming *Cucina* restaurant.

Notes: The winery's name was inspired by the miracle of Jesus turning water into wine at a wedding at Cana. (Great guy to have on your guest list, right?!)

Facts: Established 1988 • 3.1 on-site acres • Yamhill-Carlton, plus other East Washington vineyard sites); 7,000 cases annually

Owner: Gino Cuneo
Winemaker: Patrick Taylor

Date visited: _____
Went with: _____
Notes: _____
_____

view

fanciness

deck/patio

food for sale

picnic area

bus/rv

pet friendly

tours

event space

Carlo & Julian
••••••••••••••••••••••••••••••

no website yet
1000 E. Main Street; Carlton; 503.852.7432

Hours: Sat–Sun 12:00pm–5:00pm (Mem–Thanks);
Sat 12:00pm–5:00pm (off season); Closed January

Tasting Fee: FREE for 5-7 tastes

Wine: 9 varieties; $12.00-$45.00
Specializes in reds

Outside: There are two very special gardens here
– with the most adorable little tour guide ever! Five-
year-old Madeline, Felix's daughter, will show you the
fearsome attacking rooster and edible flowers too. If
you are lucky enough to catch her tour, be sure to tip
her big! To picnic, go back to the vineyards. No deck

Inside: Peaceful, eclectic, Zen-churchy space to raise
a glass in thanks to the Wine Gods and look at art.

Notes: Located about a 1/2 mile east of the "happening"
end of Carlton's Main Street. • Felix hails from
Argentina and named his winery after his two sons,
Carlo and Julian.

Facts: Established 1996 • 6 acres • Yamhill-Carlton
AVA • 1,000 cases

Owner: Felix Madrid
Winemaker: Felix Madrid

Date visited: _____
Went with: _____
Notes: _____
_____

cor

or sale

space

shop

Carlton Winemakers Studio

www.winemakersstudio.com
801 N. Scott Street; Carlton; 503.852.6100

Hours: Daily 11:00am–5:00pm (Mar–Dec);
Fri–Sun 11:00am–5:00pm (Jan–Feb)

Tasting Fee: $3.00–$20.00 flights of varying tastes,
shapes and sizes

Wine: 40 varieties; $15.00-$40.00
Specializes in hosting top Oregon winemakers

Outside: Pine trees surround the small picnic patio,
but overall, it's a facility rather than vineyard site.

Inside: Contemporary, loft-style-cool tasting room.

Notes: Sample top Oregon wines side-by-side
• LEED certified • Known as "best bang for the buck."

Facts: Established 2002 • Wines from 10 wineries

Owners: Eric Hamacher and Luisa Ponzi;
Ned and Kirsten Lumpkin

Andrew Rich—Andrew Rich
Bryce Vineyard—Bryce Bagnall
Carlton Winemakers Studio—10 vitners + own label
Domaine Meriwether—Raymond Walsh
Dominio IV Wines—Patrick Reuter
Hamacher Wines—Eric Hamacher
J. Daan Wine Cellars—Justin Van Zanten
Lazy River Vineyard— Eric Hamacher
Resonance Vineyard—Kevin Chambers
Retour Wine Co.— Eric Hamacher
Wahle Vineyards and Cellars—Mark Wahle

view

fanciness

deck/patio

food for sale

picnic area

bus/rv

pet friendly

tours

event space

Laurel Ridge

· ·

www.laurelridgewinery.com
13301 NE Kuehne Road; Carlton; 503.852.7050

Hours: Daily 12:00pm–6:00pm (wine season);
Thurs–Sun 12:00pm–5:00pm (winter)

Tasting Fee: $5.00 flight of 6 tastes (choose from 12

Wine: 12 varieties; $14.00-$25.00
Specializes in offering a broad range and value

Outside: The winery is on flat ground, peacefully
settled in the valley, surrounded by vineyard hills and
neighboring farms. Cool *old* farm equipment around.

Inside: The extra-long, open tasting room has two long
dark marble bars, and designerly touches like stained
cement, wine-colored walls and gallery photo/art.

Notes: A very wide range of wines and some of the
friendliest service in town! • Name comes from the
name of the original soil type, Laurel Loam. • Groups
are welcomed (RSVP required) and they do big outdoor weddings too.

Facts: Established 1986 (2001 present location)
• 240 acres • Yamhill-Carlton AVA • 2,250 cases

Owner: Susan Teppola
Winemakers: Chris Berg and Barnaby Tuttle

Date visited: _____
Went with: _____
Notes: _____
_____

 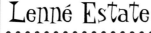

Lenné Estate
• •

www.lenneestate.com
18760 NE Laughlin Road; Yamhill; 503.956.2256

Hours: Thurs-Sun 12:00pm–5:00pm (year-round)

Tasting Fee: $5.00 flight of 4 tastes;
$5.00 for 2 tastes of Owen Roe wine

Wine: 5-6 varieties; $30.00-$45.00
Specializes in Pinot Noir

Outside: This alluring, stone, French-country barn house sits way high up on the hill, posing with charm and intrigue. The view from the large deck looking down and over the valley is gorgeous!

Inside: The tasting room has a more modern feel than the exterior, with tile floors, buttercream colored walls and wood accents surrounding the bar. Upscale in style, but simple and very warm and comfortable.

Notes: Lenné was named for Karen Lutz' father Lenny, whose profile and/or nose is on every bottle.
• Dry farming is a big part of viticulture at Lenné and an essential ingredient of their terroir.

Facts: Established 2001 • 21 acres • Yamhill-Carlton AVA • 840 cases annually

Owner: Steve Lutz
Winemaker: Steve Lutz

Date visited: _____
Went with: _____
Notes: _____
_____

view

fanciness

deck/patio

food for sale

picnic area

bus/rv

pet friendly

tours

event space

Willakenzie Estate

www.willakenzie.com
19143 NE Laughlin Road; Yamhill; 503.662.3280

Hours: Daily 12:00pm–5:00pm (year-round)

Tasting Fee: $5.00 flight of 6 tastes

Wine: 12-15 varieties; $18.00–$38.00
Specializes in Pinot varietals

Outside: Enjoy the good life! On a sunny day, it's hard to beat sitting outside Willakenzie's grand wrap-around patio. Decorative cement balusters set the stage for truly spectacular views of the vineyard.

Inside: Walk around back then straight up the steep entry staircase to enjoy wines in the light, bright and spacious European-style tasting room.

Notes: The Winery was named after the Willakenzie soil on which the vineyards were planted • Sustainable agricultural practices. • 100% estate fruit.

Facts: Established 1991 • 102 acres producing plus 300 acres natural pasture and Douglas Fir forest in Yamhill-Carlton AVA • 18,000 cases annually

Owners: Ronni and Bernard Lacroute
Winemaker: Thibaud Mandet

Date visited: _____
Went with: _____
Notes: _____
_____

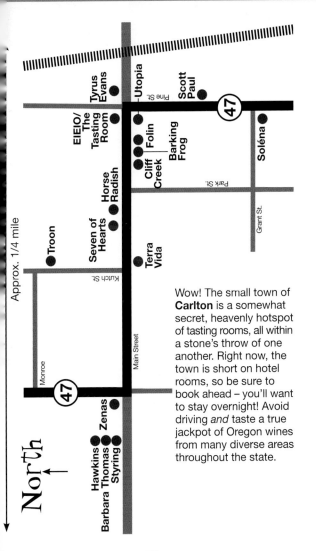

Tyrus Evans
Utopia
Scott Paul
EIEIO/ The Tasting Room
Folin
Barking Frog
Cliff Creek
Soléna
Pine St.
Park St.
Grant St.
47
Horse Radish
Seven of Hearts
Troon
Terra Vida
Kutch St.
Main Street
Monroe
47
Hawkins
Barbara Thomas
Zenas
Styring

Approx. 1/4 mile

North

Wow! The small town of **Carlton** is a somewhat secret, heavenly hotspot of tasting rooms, all within a stone's throw of one another. Right now, the town is short on hotel rooms, so be sure to book ahead – you'll want to stay overnight! Avoid driving *and* taste a true jackpot of Oregon wines from many diverse areas throughout the state.

decor

food for sale

event space

gift shop

Barking Frog

● ●

www.barkingfrogwinery.com
128 W Main Street; Carlton; 503.702.5029

Hours: Fri–Sun 1:00pm–5:00pm (summer);
Sat–Sun 1:00pm–5:00pm (off-season)

Tasting Fee: $5.00 5–6 wines

Wine: 8–10 varieties; $25–$34 average range

Notes: Inside the Barking Frog tasting room, you'll
be greeted by friendly servers and their giant, bright
green ceramic mascot. • In Native American lore,
the frog is a sign of prosperity and well-being, and
ribbets "all is right with the world." • Wine maker Ror
Helbig likes to experiment and bend some rules like
making an Ice Wine Syrah and a Sangiovese with
local grapes, and even using revolutionary Vino-Seal
wine stoppers.

Facts: Established 2005 • Sources grapes from
Willamette and Yakima Valley • 1,200 cases annually

Owner: Ron Helbig
Winemaker: Ron Helbig

Date visited: _____

Went with: _____

Notes: _____

_____

cor

or sale

space

shop

Cliff Creek

• •

www.cliffcreek.com
128 W. Main Street; Carlton; 503.852.0089

Hours: Daily 12:00pm–6:00pm (summer);
Fri–Sun 12:00pm–6:00pm (off-season)

Tasting Fee: $5.00 flight of 5 tastes

Wine: 5–6 varieties; $15.00–$30.00
Specializes in big reds like Claret and Syrah

Notes: Velvet curtains, stylish art, and fresh flowers
adorn the deep brown walls of the cozy tasting bar.
• For three generations, the Garvins have made wine
a family business. Ruth Garvin, daughter of the owners
Vern and Dorothy Garvin, is a cook with the uncanny
ability to pair wines with different foods. Garvin, owner
of Pappachino's Coffeehouse in Portland, creates
different wine pairings each month. Always be sure
to ask for more pairing ideas! • Say "Yes!" to any
cheese samples offered.

Facts: Established 2003 • 75 acres • Rogue River
Valley AVA (sister vineyard is Sam's Valley Vineyard)
• 2,500 cases annually

Owners: Vern and Dorothy Garvin (and family)
Winemaker: Joe Dobbes

Date visited: _____
Went with: _____
Notes: _____
_____

decor

food for sale

event space

gift shop

EIEIO/The Tasting Room

www.onhisfarm.com
www.pinot-noir.com
105 W. Main Street; Carlton; 503.852.6733

Hours: Daily 11:00am-5:00pm (June-Oct);
Thur-Mon 11:00am-5:00pm (Nov-May)

Tasting Fee: $10.00-$15.00 for 4-6 tastes

Wine: 13+ varieties; $25.00-$75.00 (EIEIO wines);
30-40 other local wines; $20.00-$80.00
EIEIO: Specializing in fun everyday wines
The Tasting Room: Small, NW wineries featured

Notes: The oldest tasting room in Carlton, EIEIO is
proud of its fun personality. Owner and winemaker,
Jay "Old" McDonald named his wine in the farmer
spirit: "EIEIO."• The Tasting Room is located in an
original bank from 1910. Original hard wood floors
and earthy green trim give this transformed bank a
bit of charm, but there's pretty much no attempt at
decorating the place. Be sure to browse the wines for
sale in the bank's vault (around 50 NW wines carried)

Facts: Established 1998 • Grapes collected from
various vineyards from the Willamette Valley • 800
cases annually

Owner: Jay McDonald
Winemaker: Jay McDonald

Date visited: _____
Went with: _____
Notes: _____
_____

cor

for sale

space

shop

Folin Cellars

• •

www.folincellars.com
118 W. Main Street; Carlton; 503.805.9735

Hours: Sat–Sun 1:00am-6:00pm (year-round)

Tasting Fee: FREE for 4 tastes

Wine: 4 varitites; $20.00–$30.00
Specializing in Spanish and Rhône varietals

Notes: Family owned and operated winery focusing
on making 100% Estate wines with emphasis on
handcrafted blends. • New tasting room coming August
2009 at their vineyards in Southern Oregon near
Medford on the Rogue River. • Current tasting room
in Carlton is simple in style with clean lines and black
and white accents for some added elegance. • Glass
vino-seals.

Facts: Established 2005 • 25 acres • Rogue Valley
AVA • 1,200 cases annually

Owners: Scott and Lorraine Folin; Rob Folin
Winemaker: Rob Folin

Date visited: _____
Went with: _____
Notes: _____
_____

decor

food for sale

event space

gift shop

Hawkins
• •

www.hawkinscellars.com
407 W. Main Street #3; Carlton; 503.852.3052

Hours: Fri–Mon 12:00pm–5:00pm (summer);
Sat–Sun 12:00pm–5:00pm (off-season)

Tasting Fee: FREE for 4 tastes

Wine: 4 varieties; $16.00–$24.00
Specializes in Pinot Noir

Notes: Located in the cute little threesome of country
cottages behind Zenas. Hawkins occupies an old
barbershop (and got his license cleared early as it
was not zoned residential like his neighbors').
• Tasting room is simple with a colorful palette for
a somewhat beach-like, boardwalk vibe.

Facts: Established 2007 • Sources grapes throughout
Willamette and Columbia Valleys • 800 cases

Owner: Thane Hawkins
Winemaker: Thane Hawkins

Coming soon to same location:

Barbara Thomas Wines
Styring Vineyards

Date visited: _____
Went with: _____
Notes: _____
_____

cor

or sale

space

shop

Horse Radish

The Horse Radish Cheese & Wine Bar

www.thehorseradish.com
211 W. Main Street; Carlton; 503.852.6656

Hours: Fri–Sat 12:00pm–10:00pm; Sun 1:00–6:00pm;
Mon–Thurs 12:00pm–6:00pm (hours vary seasonally)

Tasting Fee: $5.00 4–5 rotating Oregon wines

Wine: 12 bottles; 20 available by the glass

Notes: *The* place to go on Main Street for nightlife
with live music on weekend nights (check website for
calendar). • Taste a wide variety of local wines, order
a big artisan cheese plate with a glass of your favorite
beverage (they have beer and coffee too) and sink
back into one of the many comfy couches and chairs.
• Be sure to check out the rotating gallery of work
by featured artists illuminated on the old brick walls.

"Wine makes daily living easier,
less hurried, with fewer tensions
and more tolerance."

– Benjamin Franklin

Date visited: _____
Went with: _____
Notes: _____
_____

decor

food for sale

event space

gift shop

Scott Paul

• •

www.scottpaul.com
128 South Pine Street; Carlton; 503.852.7300

Hours: Fri–Sun 1:00–5:00pm (Mar–Nov);
Sat 1:00–5:00pm (Dec–Feb)

Tasting Fee: $10.00 flight of 5 tastes (varies);
Guided tastings by appointment

Wine: 4 $25.00–$40.00
Specializes in Pinot Noir

Notes: Unique opportunity to taste New World Pinot
from Oregon and Old World Pinot from Burgundy
side by side. • The tasting room is a cool, industrial-
chic, artsy space where you'll see a "Rabbit Receiving
His Own Information," the painting that inspired the
label's logo. • The circa-1915 brick tasting room was
originally a creamery. The winery occupies a building
that was a grist mill and electricity generator, and later,
a granary. • Scott is also well-known in his former life
as the east coast deejay Shadow Stevens!

Facts: Established 2005 • 30 acres in 4 vineyards
in Willamette Valley AVAs (also imports wine directly
from small family producers in Burgundy, France)
• 4,000–5,000 cases annually

Owners: Martha and Scott Wright
Winemaker: Scott Paul Wright

Date visited: _____

Went with: _____

Notes: _____

_____

cor

or sale

space

shop

Seven of Hearts

• •

www.sevenofheartswine.com
217 West Main Street; Carlton; 971.241.6548

Hours: Fri-Sun 1:00pm-6:00pm (May–Sep);
Fri-Sat 1:00pm-6:00pm (Oct-May)

Tasting Fee: $1.00 per taste (make your own flight)

Wine: 7 varieties; $18.00–$45.00
Specializes in Old World Pinot Noir

Notes: Seven of Hearts winemaker, Byron Dooley,
shares a space with wife, Dana, owner and baker
of Honest Chocolate. The tasting room is flooded
with the smell of fresh chocolate and wine (can it get
any better?) It's aromatically exhilarating! • Former
dot.com engineer turned into winemaker started his
traditional, classic-style winery to feature "old world"
techniques. A trip to Seven of Hearts tasting room
provides a unique opportunity to have a tasting with
Dooley himself. • The name Seven Of Hearts came
from their rescued cat, "Seven," who stole their hearts.

Facts: Established 2006 • 12 acres (exclusively Pinot
grapes in Yamhill-Carlton AVA) plus other Oregon
AVAs throughout the state • 900 cases annually

Owner: Byron Dooley
Winemaker: Byron Dooley

Date visited: _____
Went with: _____
Notes: _____
_____

decor

food for sale

event space

gift shop

Soléna
• •

www.solenacellars.com
213 Pine Street; Carlton; 503.852.0082

Hours: Thurs–Sun 12:00pm-5:00pm (year-round)

Tasting Fee: FREE flight of 6 tastes

Wine: 12 varieties; $16.00–$50.00
Specializes in Pinot Noir

Notes: There's love and wine behind every vine at Soléna. Owners Danielle Andrus Montalieu, daughter of a winemaker and formerly with Archery Summit, and Laurent Montalieu, grandson of a winemaker and formerly with Willakenzie, fell in love and purchased 80 acres of land as a wedding gift to themselves. Instead of registering for china and blenders, this couple asked for varieties of Pinot Noir vines as wedding gifts. • Soléna is the combination of the Spanish and French words "Solana" and "Solene" celebrating the sun and the moon, and the name that Laurent and Danielle gave to their daughter. • Inside the long living-room-like tasting room, don't miss the beautiful wood wine bar handcarved by Laurent's father.

Facts: Established 2000 • 80 acres • Yamhill-Carlton AVA (plus more in East Washington) • 5,000 cases

Owners: Danielle and Laurent Montalieu
Winemaker: Laurent Montalieu

Date visited: _____
Went with: _____
Notes: _____
_____

cor

or sale

space

shop

Terra Vina

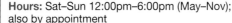

www. terravinawines.com
214 'B' W. Main Street; Carlton; 503.852.6777

Hours: Sat–Sun 12:00pm–6:00pm (May–Nov);
also by appointment

Tasting Fee: $5.00 for 6+ tastes

Wine: 15 varieties; $18.00-$36.00
Specializes in big, bold reds

Notes: Cute tasting room done up in small-town,
charming café-style with brick walls and country flair.
• Formerly Dalla Vina Wines, this award-winning wine
is crafted at the Owen Roe Winery. • Terra Vina means
"wine of the land" in Italian. Their byline: "Respecting
the Earth, Creating Great Wine." • Located next-door
to Cuvee restaurant, *the* fine-dining spot in town and
not to be missed!

Facts: Established 2005 • 9 acres • Chehalem
Mountains AVA (plus sources grapes from Columbia
Valley AVA) • 2,000 cases annually

Owners: Carole and Karl Dinger
Winemaker: Karl Dinger

Date visited: _____
Went with: _____
Notes: _____
_____

decor

food for sale

event space

gift shop

Troon

• •

www.troonvineyard.com
250 N. Kutch Street; Carlton; 503.852.3084

Hours: Daily 11:00am–6:00pm (summer);
Fri–Mon 11:00am–5:00pm (off-season)

Tasting Fee: $5.00 for 5 tastes (free first taste)

Wine: 25 varieties; $18.00–$25.00
Specializes in Cab, Zinfandel and blends

Notes: Gorgeous and well-done interior with huge,
old, gnarly grapevine for display and effect. Traditional
and rich, old-world decor. • They take a natural
approach to wine-making and use sustainable farming
methods. • Summertime fun goes until 6:00pm.
Warmer weather also brings live music to the back
patio on Saturdays 4:00pm–7:00pm with wines by
the glass too. • Unique "Vermentino White" and don't
miss the infamous "Druid's Fluid". • Light snacks, like
hummus or cheese plates, available for purchase.
• Also visit them at the vineyard/winery in Grants Pass

Facts: Established 2003 (1972 plantings) • 100 acres
(33 planted plus sourced grapes) • Applegate Valley
AVA • 7,500 cases annually

Owners: The Martin Family (originally established
by Dick Troon)
Winemaker: Herb Quady

Date visited: _____
Went with: _____
Notes: _____
_____

cor

or sale

space

shop

Tyrus Evan

• •

www.tyrusevan.com
120 Pine Street; Carlton; 503.852.7010

Hours: Daily 11:00am-6:00pm (May-Sep);
Daily 11:00am-5:00pm (Oct-Apr); Fri–Sat 'til 6:00pm

Tasting Fee: $10.00 for 6 tastes; with an optional
cheese plate for $5.00

Wine: 6 varieties; $25.00-$40.00
Specializing in warm climate varietals

Notes: Original 1921 train station that has been
restored to the finest detail. The front of the tasting room
has a covered picnic area surrounded by beautifully
landscaped grounds. Warm woods with olive and
brick-red tones tie this western-themed train station
into a fun, unique tasting room! Equipped with both
a classy, tall tasting bar and lush chairs to truly
enjoy your tasting experience. • Famed Pinot Noir
winemaker, Ken Wright, began this label to make
varieties. • Named for Ken Wright's sons, Cody and
Carson, using their middle names.

Facts: Established 2001 • Grapes from warmer areas
of Southern OR and Eastern WA • 5,000 cases

Owner: Ken Wright
Winemaker: Ken Wright

Date visited: _____
Went with: _____
Notes: _____
_____

decor

food for sale

event space

gift shop

Utopia

• •

www.utopiawine.com
116 W. Main Street; Carlton; 503.852.7546

Hours: Sat–Sun 1:00pm–5:00pm (year-round)

Tasting Fee: $5.00 flight of 4 tastes

Wine: 4 varieties; $25.00-$45.00
Specializing in organic Pinot Noir

Notes: Owner and winemaker Daniel Warnshuis'
lifelong dream was for his own vineyard. In fact, it
was his idea of "Utopia." His beautiful vineyard site is
in Ribbon Ridge. The tasting room is built in Carlton's
original movie theater. • On the weekends, Warnshuis
sometimes adds a "mystery taste"—how good are
your wine taste buds? • The wine shop here has
well-stocked shelves of mysteries and surprises too!

Facts: Established 2005 • 18 acres • Ribbon Ridge
Appellation AVA • 800 cases annually

Owner: Daniel Warnshuis
Winemaker: Daniel Warnshuis

"Wine... cheereth God and man."

– Judges, 9:13

Date visited: _____
Went with: _____
Notes: _____
_____

cor

/
or sale

space

shop

Zenas

● ●

www.zenaswines.com
407 W. Main Street; Carlton; 503.852.3000

Hours: Sat–Sun 12:00pm-5:00pm (year-round)

Tasting Fee: $10.00 for 4+ wines (and you get to keep the Zenas wine glass)

Wine: 4 varieties; $19.00–$33.00
Specializing in Bordeaux-style wines

Notes: Once an old Nash car dealership, this tasting room still shows original features, including the extra-low windows that were originally used to showcase the hot cars. • Named after Howard Zenas, who came to Oregon via the Oregon Trail in 1856. Now, five generations later, his family honors his pioneering triumphs through wine.

Facts: Established 2004 • Grapes sourced from Yamhill-Carlton and Rogue River AVAs • 800 cases

Owners: The Howard Family
Winemakesr: Blake and Kevin Howard

Date visited: _____
Went with: _____
Notes: _____
_____

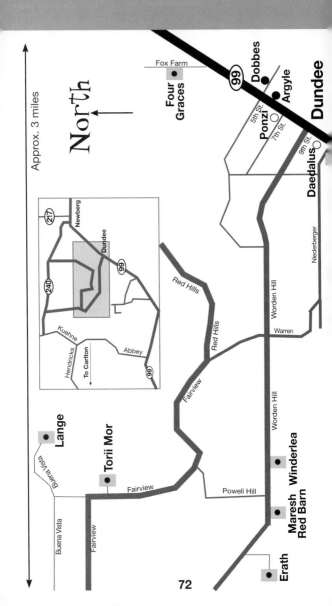

North

Approx. 3 miles

Fox Farm

99

Dobbes

Argyle

Dundee

Four Graces

5th St.

Ponzi

7th St.

9th St.

Daedalus

Niederberger

Newberg

217

Dundee

99

240

Red Hills

Worden Hill

Kuehne

Abbey

Warren

Hendricks

To Carlton

99

Red Hills

Lange

Fairview

Buena Vista

Torii Mor

Worden Hill

Fairview

Powell Hill

Maresh

Winderlea

Red Barn

Buena Vista

Fairview

Erath

72

Dundee Hills — South

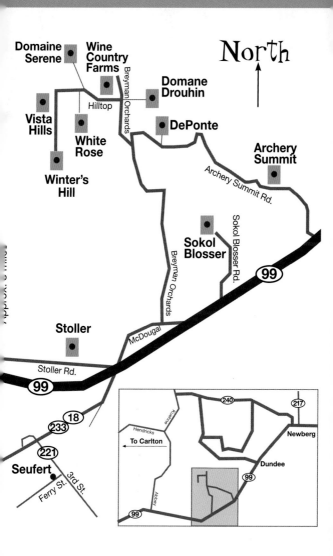

North

Domaine Serene
Wine Country Farms
Breyman Orchards
Domane Drouhin
Hilltop
DePonte
Vista Hills
White Rose
Archery Summit
Archery Summit Rd.
Winter's Hill
Sokol Blosser
Sokol Blosser Rd.
Breyman Orchards
99
Stoller
McDougal
Stoller Rd.
99
18
233
221
Seufert
3rd St.
Ferry St.

240
217
Kuehne
Hendricks
To Carlton
Newberg
Abbey
Dundee
99
99

Photos © Andrea Johnson

PREMIER CUVÉE

view

fanciness

deck/patio

food for sale

picnic area

bus/rv

pet friendly

tours

event space

Archery Summit

• •

www.archerysummit.com
18599 NE Archery Summit; Dayton; 503.864.4300

Hours: Daily 10:00am–4:00pm (year-round)

Tasting Fee: $15.00 flight of 4 Pinot tastes

Wine: 5 varieties; $48.00-$85.00
Specializes in single-vineyard Pinot Noir

Outside: Highly impressive from the entrance gate and beyond. The paved road and elegant drive up leads to their commanding hilltop positioning, giving them high marks by one and all. What a *view!* Tastings only (no bottles or wines by the glass allowed in or out)

Inside: Tasting room is surprisingly small with a marble bar and rich, dark, woods. The winery has five floors and includes a fascinating barrel-lined cave hallway and not-to-be-missed bathrooms. Really!

Notes: Unpretentious elegance and a movement toward friendlier staff. • Tours at 10:30am and 2:00pm for $25.00 including tastings. Very reputable wines overall (served for several presidents).

Facts: Established 1993 • 120 acres • Dundee Hills and Ribbon Ridge AVAs • 10,000 cases annually

Owners: Crimson Wine Group
Winemaker: Anna Matzinger

Date visited: _____
Went with: _____
Notes: _____
_____

Argyle

• •

www.argylewinery.com
691 Highway 99W; Dundee; 503.538.8520

Hours: Daily 11:00am–5:00pm (year-round)

Tasting Fee: $8.00–$10.00 flight of 4-5 tastes

Wine: 12 varieties; $25.00-$45.00
Specializes in Sparklings and Pinot Noir

Notes: Argyle is very conveniently positioned right off 99W at the north end of Dundee. • Enter through the lush gardens onto the quaint, white, wooden deck and into the tasting room. The interior matches the exterior in historic tone and period style, done up in relaxing, neutral tones with a long tasting bar. Events take place in adjacent operating winery. • The bottle labels stem from the Scottish argyle-diamond shape. • LIVE and Salmon-Safe certified. • The winemaker has been ranked seven times among the Top 100 Wines of the World by Wine Spectator.

Facts: Established 1987 • Sources grapes from all over the Willamette Valley and Eola-Amilty Hills • 45,000 cases annually

Owner: Rollin Soles
Winemaker: Rollin Soles

Date visited: _____
Went with: _____
Notes: _____
_____

view

fanciness

deck/patio

food for sale

picnic area

bus/rv

pet friendly

tours

event space

De Ponte Cellars

www.depontecellars.com
17545 Archery Summit Road; Dayton; 503.864.3698

Hours: Daily 11:00am–5:00pm (year-round)

Tasting Fee: $10.00 flight of 3-4 tastes

Wine: 4–5 varieties; $24.00–$45.00
Specializes in Burgundian-style wines

Outside: Valley views plus glimpses of Mt. Hood and Mt. Jefferson greet you along with the rolling hills and vines. Walk into the stylish, rust-colored barn to the tasting room, then out to the bistro tables on the patio

Inside: Spanish touches like arches, tiles, rugs and wrought iron accents create a cozy ambiance. The back tasting bar has deep wood cabinets and an upscale homey kitchen look.

Notes: Low-key and relaxed, this family boutique winery is famous for their Melon wine style. The name De Ponte comes from the matriarch/grandmother of the Baldwin family, Shirley Baldwin. De Ponte, her maiden name, is of Portuguese decent.

Facts: Established 1999 • 15 acres • Dundee Hills AVA • 2500-3000 cases annually

Owners: Shirley Baldwin / Baldwin Family
Winemaker: Isabelle Dutarte

Date visited: _____
Went with: _____
Notes: _____
_____

cor

or sale

space

shop

Dobbes Family Estate

www.dobbesfamilyestate.com
www.winebyjoe.com
240 SE 5th Street; Dundee; 503.538.1141

Hours: Daily 11:00am–6:00pm (year-round)

Tasting Fee: FREE flight of 2 tastes (Wine by Joe);
$10.00 premium flight of 5 tastes (Dobbes Family
Estate)

Wine: 17 varieties all together; $10.00-$65.00
Specializes in Pinot Noir and Pinot Gris

Notes: The nicely landscaped entrance here leads
into a well thought-out tasting room wrapped around
a huge cedar tree trunk "growing" in the center of the
room • Hint: If you're heading back to Portland after
a day in wine country, stop here and let the rush
hour pass—they are open until 6:00pm • Tune in
weekly: "Northwest Vine Time" airs every Saturday
from 4:00pm–5:00pm on Portland's KXL Newsradio
750AM, featuring Joe Dobbes. Joe consults for as
many as 20 wineries (www.joethewinemaker.com).

Facts: Established 2005 • 214 acres • Willamette
Valley and Eola Hills/Amity AVAs, plus select vineyards throughout Oregon • 25,000 cases annually

Owner: Joe Dobbes
Winemaker: Joe Dobbes

Date visited: _____
Went with: _____
Notes: _____
_____

view

fanciness

deck/patio

food for sale

picnic area

bus/rv

pet friendly

tours

event space

Domaine Drouhin

www.domainedrouhin.com
6750 Breyman Orchards Road; Dayton; 503.864.2700

Hours: Wed–Sun 11:00am–4:00pm

Tasting Fee: $10.00 flight of 3 tastes

Wine: 4 varieties; $30.00–$65.00
Specializes in Pinot Noir

Outside: Absolutely gorgeous! This is a true highlight on any tour. Open lawn area and lush, landscaped grounds. The covered patio denies you the view of Mt. Hood (otherwise you would never leave!)

Inside: Majestic and fancy! Tasting bar is on the upper level of a huge room with vaulted ceiling and windows. Downstairs, get more elbow room, peek through the windows to the production area, and enjoy the views.

Notes: Founded in 1880 in Beaune, France by Maison Joseph Drouhin. • This is a fourth generation family business with a proud history and literally deep roots in Oregon. • RSVP for a private and informative walk-through 60-minute tour with wine and cheeses.

Facts: Established 1988 • 225 acres (100 planted) • Dundee Hills AVA • 17,000 cases annually

Owner: Robert Drouhin
Winemaker: Veronique Drouhin

Date visited: _____
Went with: _____
Notes: _____
_____

Domaine Serene

....

www.domaineserene.com
6555 NE Hilltop Lane; Dayton; 866.864.6555

Hours: Wed–Sun 11:00am–4:00pm (year-round)

Tasting Fee: $15.00 flight of 4 tastes

Wine: 8-10 varieties; $35.00–$90.00
Specializes in Pinot Noir and Chardonnay

Outside: Another "Domaine" that is also spectacular! The paved drive up is reminiscent of the Tuscan country-side with rolling hills and the distant Italian-style estate with its terra cotta roof. This is *the* place to bring guests.

Inside: Wow! A most magnificent and stately tasting room with Italian marble floors, giant windows, and oversized fireplace. Armoires, antiques and chande-liers bring old world elegance to Oregon.

Notes: Named for Serene, the Evenstad's daughter.
• RSVP for the VIP private tour package ($40.00) with sit-down tastings, cheese pairings and full tour.
• You'll want to picnic, but the bees in the 'hood will most likely find you fast and ruin that plan.

Facts: Established 1989 • 150 acres (planted)
• Dundee Hills AVA • 20,000 cases annually

Owners: Ken and Grace Evenstad
Winemaker: Eleni Papadakis

Date visited: _____
Went with: _____
Notes: _____

view

fanciness

deck/patio

food for sale

picnic area

bus/rv

pet friendly

tours

event space

Duck Pond

• •

www.duckpondcellars.com
23145 Highway 99W; Dundee; 503.538.3199

Hours: Daily 10:00am–5:00pm (May–Sep);
Daily 11:00am–5:00pm (Oct–Apr)

Tasting Fee: FREE Basic (4-5); $5.00 Premium (4-5)

Wine: 8-10 varieties; $10.00–$18.00
Specializes in affordable variety

Outside: Right off Hwy 99 and one of the first places you'll see when coming from Portland. Sprawling, flat, front lawn great for picnics. Find the giant, octagonal wooden party deck or plant yourself at a café table in the sweet garden area just outside the tasting room.

Inside: Friendly, country-plantation charm with white wooden, overhead trellised entry, a huge warehouse party space and one of wine country's best gift shops.

Notes: Check calendar for fun summertime events including parties, bands, dinners and festivals.
• Lots of room to run and play and a duck pond too!

Facts: Established 1993 • 325 acres in Willamette Valley near Salem and 520 in Washington's Columbia Valley AVA • 125,000+ cases annually

Owners: The Fries and Jenkins families
Winemaker: Mark Chargin

Date visited: _____
Went with: _____
Notes: _____

Erath

● ●

www.erath.com
9409 NE Worden Hill Road; Dundee; 800.539.9463

Hours: Daily 11:00am–5:00pm (year-round)

Tasting Fee: FREE flight of 3 tastes; $10.00 and/or
$15.00 for premium flights of 4 tastes

Wine: 11 varieties; $10.00–$50.00
Specializes in Pinot Noir

Outside: The tasting room is located in the former
home of Oregon Wine Pioneer, Dick Erath. It has a
golden, log cabin-like exterior and a large patio out
front overlooking the vineyard. The other end of the
building has a second deck area with views and lots
of tables.

Inside: Inside the tasting room you'll find a long and
very popular bar! Lots of polished wood and windows.

Notes: Erath is owned by Ste. Michelle Wine Estates.
• They don't do events per se, but there are a lot of
outdoor tables that can accommodate groups.

Facts: Established 1969 • 118 acres • Dundee Hills
AVA plus purchases grapes from another 130 acres
in Oregon • 65,000 cases produced annually

Owner: Dick Erath
Winemaker: Gary Horner

Date visited: _____
Went with: _____
Notes: _____
_____

view

fanciness

deck/patio

food for sale

picnic area

bus/rv

pet friendly

tours

event space

Four Graces

• •

www.thefourgraces.com
9605 NE Fox Farm Road; Dundee; 800.245.2950

Hours: Daily 10:00am–5:00pm (year-round)

Tasting Fees: $10.00 flight of 5 tastes

Wine: 5-6 varieties; $18.00–$42.00
Specializes in Pinot Noir, Pinot Blanc and Pinot Gris

Outside: Right out the back door of this charming home lies a pleasant vista of vines and hills, up close and personal. Enjoy the outdoor patio and brick fireplace for the ultimate in relaxation.

Inside: The interior of this well-decorated, small cottage is gracefully furnished in black and white, with framed black- and-white photographs. Chic and sophisticated, charming yet urban-eclectic inside. Cute and homey.

Notes: Winery gets its name from the owners' four daughters (there's also one son). They are LIVE and Salmon-Safe certified, and practice sustainable and biodynamic farming. • Event space for up to 30.

Facts: Established 2003 (1993 vines) • 110 acres • Dundee Hills •14,000 cases annually

Owners: Steven and Paula Black
Winemaker: Laurent Montalieu

Date visited: _____
Went with: _____
Notes: _____
_____

Lange Estate

www.langewinery.com
18380 NE Buena Vista Road; Dundee; 503.538.6476

Hours: Daily 11:00am–5:00pm (year-round)

Tasting Fee: $10.00 flight of 4–5 tastes

Wine: 12 varieties; $15.00-$60.00
Specializes in Pinot Noir, Pinot Gris and Chardonnay

Outside: It's all about the spectacular view here!
Grab your sweetheart and nab that romantic, little
two-seater bench at the edge of paradise, overlooking two valleys with views of Mt. Hood and Mt.
Jefferson. A small lawn and summer patio are just
outside the quaint, white-sided house.

Inside: The tasting room is simple and white with two
tasting bars and nice cherry wood furnishings. A vaulted
ceiling, big windows and an interesting concrete floor
with wood inlay make the room feel larger.

Notes: Lange Estate Winery is LIVE certified • A little
mnemonic device to help you remember where to
come back to: "Dang! Lange has great views!"

Facts: Established 1987 • 45 acres • Dundee Hills
AVA • 16,000 cases annually

Owners: Don and Wendy Lange
Winemakers: Don Lange and Jesse Lange

Date visited: _____
Went with: _____
Notes: _____
_____

view

fanciness

deck/patio

food for sale

picnic area

bus/rv

pet friendly

tours

event space

Maresh Red Barn
• •

www.vineyardretreat.com
9325 NE Worden Hill Road; Dundee; 503.537.1098

Hours: Wed–Sun 11:00am–5:00pm (Mar–Nov only)

Tasting Fee: $5.00 flight of 4 tastes

Wine: 3-5 varieties; $15.00-$50.00
Specializes in Pinot Noir

Outside: You'll recognize and remember this landmark smack-dab in the middle of Dundee Hills. The big red barn sits amongst the vines and rolling hills and offers picnickers stellar views of Mt. Hood and Mt. Jefferson.

Inside: Nice view from the back deck of tasting room too! Casual and friendly farmhouse feel with recycled basketball court floors. Cheese, crackers, and chocolate nibbles are usually provided on weekends.

Notes: Currently have their Maresh Label on wines by Archery Summit, J. Christopher and 12th & Maple Wines. • One of the very first vineyards established in Oregon (fifth in the state). • Pronounced "Marsh," a Slavic surname. • Retreat center/house next door.

Facts: Established 1970 • 50 acres • Dundee Hills AVA • 6,000 cases annually

Owners: Jim and Loie Maresh
Winemakers: Various local winemakers

Date visited: _____
Went with: _____
Notes: _____
_____

Seufert

Seufert

● ●

www.seufertwinery.com
415 Ferry Street; Dayton; 503.709.1255

Hours: Sat–Sun 12:00pm–5:00pm (wine season);
By appointment only (winter)

Tasting Fee: FREE flight of 3-5 tastes

Wine: 12 varieties; $15.00–$45.00
Specializes in Pinot Noir

Notes: The Seufert winery is a small operation with
a bright future, if not such a long history. The tasting
room and the winery are on the main street in downtown Dayton. This is a bare-bones facility with no
thought given to decor per se, but a perfect place
to learn about and sample the nuances of individual
Willamette Valley AVAs. • Make sure to have Jim, or one
of the lovely and super-friendly wine-istas, explain
how a biodynamic wine is grown! • Jim Seufert
(pronounced "SIGH-fert") also developed the brilliant
"Wine Snapshot," a labeling system that illustrates
wine characteristics and food pairing suggestions.

Facts: Established 2005 • Sources grapes from 5 of
the 6 Willamette Valley AVAs • 2,000 cases annually

Owner: Jim Seufert
Winemaker: Jim Seufert

Date visited: _____
Went with: _____
Notes: _____
_____

Sokol Blosser

view

fanciness

deck/patio

food for sale

picnic area

bus/rv

pet friendly

tours

event space

Sokol Blosser

• •

www.sokolblosser.com
5000 Sokol Blosser Lane; Dundee; 503.864.2282

Hours: Daily 10:00am–4:00pm (year-round)

Tasting Fee: $5-$15 (different flights)

Wine: 10 varieties; $15.00–$40.00
Specializes in Pinot Noir; also releases under widely-recognized *Meditrina* and *Evolution* labels

Outside: Walk up to the upscale-rustic gray barn-house and enjoy views of Mt. Hood and Mt. Jefferson (on a clear day). Bring a snack and have a picnic at one of several table areas in the front or back.

Inside: Sip at the large, central bar with 180° views through giant windows and modern vaulted ceiling with exposed wood beams.

Notes: Friendly & down-to-earth attitude. Dedicated to sustainable and environmentally-friendly practices (LEED certified). Pet-friendly. One of the most active wineclubs in Oregon. RSVP for a great tour Fri–Sun offered at 10:00am and 12:00pm for only $10.00.

Facts: Established 1971 (one of Oregon's oldest)
• 100 acres • Dundee Hills AVA • 85,000 cases

Owners: Bill Blosser and Susan Sokol Blosser
Winemaker: Russ Rosner

Date visited: _____
Went with: _____
Notes: _____
_____

© 2008 Mike Haverkate

Stoller

• •

www.stollervineyards.com
16161 NE McDougall Road; Dayton; 503.864.3404

Hours: Daily 11:00am–5:00pm (year-round)

Tasting Fee: $10.00 flight of 3–5 tastes

Wine: 5 varieties; $17.00-$40.00
Specializes in Pinot Noir and Chardonnay

Outside: This is *the* place to come for that incredible Mt. Hood view! Originally a huge turkey farm, now a state-of-the-art winery. Lots of lawn space!

Inside: This very contemporary, gallery-like tasting room gives you a large glass table and artsy chairs to sit and really enjoy the tasting. The large windows open up the space and allow a great view of the vineyard and Mt. Hood.

Notes: The Stoller Winery was built with the environment in mind, being LEED-Gold, LIVE and Salmon-Safe certified. Enjoy their 9-hole disc golf course and picnic-perfect pasture. Big outdoor event space.

Facts: Established 1995 • 373 acres • Dundee Hills AVA • 10,000 cases annually

Owners: Bill and Cathy Stoller
Winemaker: Melissa Burr

ew

iness

/patio

for sale

ic area

us/rv

riendly

ours

t space

Date visited: _____
Went with: _____
Notes: _____

view

fanciness

deck/patio

food for sale

picnic area

bus/rv

pet friendly

tours

event space

Torii Mor

• •

www.toriimorwinery.com
18325 NE Fairview Road; Dundee; 800.839.5004

Hours: Daily 11:00am–5:00pm (year-round)

Tasting Fee: $10.00 flight of 7 tastes

Wine: 12 varieties; $20.00–$60.00;
Specializes in Pinot Noir

Outside: The best of the West meets East with gorgeous Oregon wine country views and a Japanese-style garden, highlighted by a beautiful namesake gate. The surrounding orchards and vineyards will have a calming effect on even the busiest Type-A personality. Relax, enjoy the view, and bong the gong!

Inside: The tasting room reflects Japanese pagoda styling with calming, simple and comfortable design.

Notes: Torii Mor means "gateway to the earth" ("torii" refers to the ornate gates at the entrances to Japanese gardens and "mor" is a word in ancient Scandinavian that means "earth").

Facts: Established 1993 • 11 acres • Dundee Hills (plus other grapes from over ten select vineyards) • 16,000 cases annually

Owners: Don Olson, MD and his wife, Margie
Winemaker: Jacques Tardy

Date visited: _____
Went with: _____
Notes: _____
_____

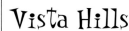

Vista Hills
• •

www.vistahillsvineyard.com
6475 Hilltop Lane; Dayton; 503.864.3200

Hours: Daily 12:00pm–5:00pm (year-long)

Tasting Fees: $10.00 flight of 4 tastes

Wine: 5-6 varieties; $18.00–$44.00
Specializes in Pinot Noir and Pinot Gris

Outside: This place is a stunner! Offering spectacular views of the valley and Cascade mountain range, the tasting room hideout sits way up high and towers over many hills and vistas.

Inside: Giant windows everywhere give you a true feeling of being in a "tree house." Elegant but rustic, ski lodge feeling. Comfy chairs and a fireplace make it a phenomenal place to watch a sunset in the winter!

Notes: Cooperative "custom crush" agreement with guest winemakers and grapes involving Panther Creek, White Rose and Arcane Cellars • Party space for up to 80 guests inside (250 for weddings and events outside) • LIVE and Salmon-Safe certified.

Facts: Established 2007 (1997 vines) • 42 acres • Dundee Hills AVA • 2,500 cases annually

Owners: John and Nancy McClintock
Winemaker: Dave Petterson

Date visited: _____
Went with: _____
Notes: _____
_____

ew

iness

/patio

or sale

c area

s/rv

riendly

urs

space

view

fanciness

deck/patio

food for sale

picnic area

bus/rv

pet friendly

tours

event space

White Rose

• •

www.whiterosewines.com
6250 NE Hilltop Lane; Dayton; 503.864.2328

Hours: Daily 11:00am–5:00pm (May–Nov);
Sat–Sun 11:00am–5:00pm (Dec–Apr)

Tasting Fees: $10.00 flight of 4 tastes

Wine: 4 varieties; $25.00–$50.00
Specializes in Pinot Noir

Outside: Wow! Absolutely spectacular view! They are actually *above* the Vista Hills treehouse.

Inside: The tasting room is inside the winery building, so it's nothing fancy, but designerly attention to detail was paid to paint color, doors, flooring, etc.

Notes: Named by previous owners after all the white roses on the grounds. Now, visit in the summer to see (and smell) all the lavender! • Author's note: I have to proclaim that I love this wine and am moved to exclaim, "Thank you, Jesus!" He's got some miraculous wine.

Facts: Established 2004 (late 70's and 80's vines) • 10 on-site acres (plus sources grapes from nearby neighbors) • Dundee Hills AVA • 2,500 cases

Owner: Greg Sanders
Winemaker: Jesus Guillen, Jr.

Date visited: _____
Went with: _____
Notes: _____

Winderlea

• •

www.winderlea.com
8905 NE Worden Hill Road; Dundee; 503.554.5900

Hours: Fri–Sun 11:00am–4:00pm (wine season)

Tasting Fees: $10.00 flight of 4-6 tastes
Full tasting fee is donated to Salud!

Wine: 6 varieties; $30.00–$50.00
Specializes in Pinot Noir

Outside: Very contemporary, modern building set right in the middle of the Red Hills of Dundee with full views in every direction. Winderlea is wonderful!

Inside: Sleek, industrial, gallery-like interior with glass walls that frame the expansive wine country gorgeousness from above. Giant garage door windows open up to the wind and sun on nice summer days.

Notes: Windows! • Winderlea (Win-dur-lee) is a loose translation of "valley protected from the wind" and is considered a safe and happy haven. • Lunches on Fridays in the summer with reservations (Jul–Sep).

Facts: Established 2006 • 20 acres (1974 plantings) Dundee Hills AVA (plus sourced grapes from the Chehalem and McMinnville AVAs) • 1,600 cases

Owners: Bill Sweat and Donna Morris
Winemaker: Robert Brittan

Date visited: _____
Went with: _____
Notes: _____
_____

view

fanciness

deck/patio

food for sale

picnic area

bus/rv

pet friendly

tours

event space

Wine Country Farm

www.winecountryfarm.com
6855 Breyman Orchards Road; Dayton; 503.864.3446

Hours: Daily 11:00am–5:00pm (wine season);
Sat-Sun 11:00am-5:00pm (Dec–May)

Tasting Fees: $5.00 flight of 5 tastes

Wine: 6 varieties; $12.00–$30.00
Specializes in Pinot and Muller-Thurgau

Outside: Well, it's just super cute here! And the views are to-die-for sweeping and spectacular! In fact, it's a recommended stop in the "1,000 Places to See Before You Die" book. Plus, there are several super-sweet areas to sit, relax, and take it all in.

Inside: Find the tasting room outer door sign and enter through the Tuscan-style hall with tasting bar. The adjacent party room has plenty of café seating plus a cozy fireplace lounging area. Perfect patio too!

Notes: They do weddings, arrange horse-drawn buggy rides (horseback tours too), and have a B&B.

Facts: Established 2005 • 25 acres (9 acres with 1970 plantings) • Dundee Hills AVA • 1,000 cases

Owner: Joan Davenport
Winemaker: Alberto Alcazar

Date visited: _____
Went with: _____
Notes: _____

Winter's Hill

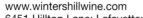

www.wintershillwine.com
6451 Hilltop Lane; Lafayette; 503.864.4538

Hours: Daily 12:00pm–5:00pm (May–Oct);
Friday thru Sunday 12:00pm–5:00pm (Dec–Apr)

Tasting Fee: $10.00 flight of 6 tastes

Wine: 12-14 varieties; $15.00–$39.00
Specializes in Pinot Noir, Pinot Gris and Muscat

Outside: Bring your binoculars! Southern views plus
a birding/hiking trail. The natural flora is marked so
you can identify the wildflowers and poison oak in
the 15 acres of Fish and Wildlife forest preserve.

Inside: Very simple barn/garage-style tasting room
with a small, three-sided tasting bar. Wildlife prints
and a small array of delicious, locally-produced snack
items available for purchase. Needs bigger windows!

Notes: Named after the owner's family name,
"Winter," this namesake is also appropriate as
Winter's Hill feels a touch remote and is a step away
from modern society in its simplicity and respect for
nature and the land.

Facts: Established 2000 (1990 plantings) • 170 acres
(36 planted in Dundee-Hills AVA • 3,000–5,000 cases

Owners: Peter and Emily Gladhart
Winemaker: Delphine Gladhart

Date visited: _____
Went with: _____
Notes: _____
_____

McMinnville

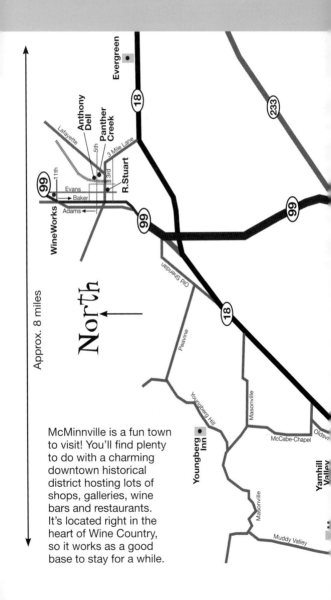

Approx. 8 miles

North

Evergreen

18

233

Anthony
Dell

Panther
Creek

Lafayette

5th

3 Mile Lane

11th

99

3rd

R. Stuart

Evans

Baker

Adams

WineWorks

99

99

Old Sheridan

18

Peavine

Youngberg Hill

Masonville

Youngberg
Inn

McCabe-Chapel

Oldsvi

Yamhill
Valley

Masonville

Muddy Valley

McMinnville is a fun town
to visit! You'll find plenty
to do with a charming
downtown historical
district hosting lots of
shops, galleries, wine
bars and restaurants.
It's located right in the
heart of Wine Country,
so it works as a good
base to stay for a while.

Anthony Dell

●●●●●●●●●●●●●●●●●●●●●●●●●●●●●

www.anthonydellcellars.com
845 NE 5th St; Suite 300; McMinnville; 503.910.8874

Hours: Fri-Sun 12:00pm–5:00pm (Mem–Thanks)

Tasting Fee: $5.00 for 4-6 tastes

Wine: 4-6 varieties; $16.00–$28.00
Specializes in small, boutique wine-making

Notes: Located in the historic heart of downtown
McMinnville, Anthony Dell Cellars tasting room is
situated in a large, working warehouse. • This Ma & Pa
winery has a relaxed feel with a cozy wine bar within
the wine processing area. • Anthony Dell Cellars
derives its name from the middle names of the two
founders • Recent label change (see above). • Proud
to be very connected to the community.

Facts: Established 2002 • 3 acres • Willamette Valley
AVA along with other grapes sourced from throughout
the state • 1,000 cases annually

Owners: Douglas Anthony Drawbond & Joy Dell Means
Winemaker: Douglas Anthony Drawbond

Date visited: _____
Went with: _____
Notes: _____

Eyrie Vineyards

decor

food for sale

event space

gift shop

www.eyrievineyards.com
935 NE 10th Avenue; McMinnville; 888.440.4970

Hours: Wed-Sun 12:00pm–5:00pm (closed January)

Tasting Fee: $5.00 Flight of 5–7 tastes

Wine: 9 varieties; $18.00–$33.00
Specializes in Pinot Noir and Pinot Gris

Notes: The Eyrie Vineyards is home to the first Pinot Noir in the Willamette Valley and the first Pinot Gris in America! In 1975, The Eyrie Vineyards produced the first American Pinot Noir to compete successfully with Burgundy. (Paris, 1979; Beaune, 1980.) David Lett (affectionately known as "Papa Pinot"), was clearly a pioneer and his legacy is safe in the hands of his son Jason Lett. The name "Eyrie" is pronounced EYE-ree and comes from a Gaelic translation of "hawks nest," as Red-tail hawks nest in an enormous fir tree at the top of the of the vineyard. The renovated, simple and quaint Eyrie tasting room is attached to the winery, and presents an array of historical pictures and articles to check out while tasting.

Facts: Established 1966 (1970 first vintage) • 50 acres • Dundee Hills AVA • 8,000–10,000 cases annually

Owners: The David Lett family
Winemaker: Jason Lett

Date visited: _____
Went with: _____
Notes: _____
_____

cor

space

or sale

hop

Evergreen Vineyards
• •

www.evergreenvineyards.com
3850 Three Mile Lane; McMinnville; 866.434.4818

Hours: Daily 11:00am–5:00pm (year-round)

Tasting Fee: FREE flight of 5-6 tastings

Wine: 11 varieties; $15.00–$30.00
Specializes in Pinot Noir—and fun labels too

Notes: A very unique place for tasting! There are
tasting rooms in both the Aviation and Space Museums,
so you can make a day of it or just sample and enjoy
the satellites, fighter jets, rockets, capsules and even
the famous Spruce Goose overhead. There's an
IMAX theater there as well, rounding out this site as
one of Oregon's top tourist attractions. The tasting
bars themselves are quite small, but there are lots of
tables around to sit, relax, and take a load off. The
gift shop has many small sweets, snacks, and goodies,
but if you want a full lunch, you can head to the
Guckenheimer Café. Some cool aviator gifts flying
around too.

Facts: Established 2002 (planted 1989) • 250 acres
• McMinnville AVA • 8,000–9,000 cases annually

Owner: Delford M. Smith
Winemaker: Laurent Montalieu

Date visited: _____
Went with: _____
Notes: _____
_____

view

fanciness

deck/patio

food for sale

picnic area

bus/rv

pet friendly

tours

event space

Maysara

• •

www.maysara.com
15765 SW Muddy Valley; McMinnville; 503.843.1234

Hours: Mon–Sat 12:00pm–5:00pm (year-round)

Tasting Fee: $7.00 flight of 6+ tastes

Wine: 9 varieties; $16.00-$50.00
Specializes in Pinot Noir

Outside: Get out your hiking boots to get the best views—and bring your bike too! The photo album on their website willl show how a hike to the top of the vineyard is worth the trip, but if you're in relaxation mode, it's cool to just hang out, sip and relax.

Inside: A large tree stump has been turned into an interesting tasting bar in the front end of the winery. Simple garage-style interior open to the barrel room.

Notes: Maysara means "house of wine" in Persian. Maysara is the largest biodynamic vineyard in the northwest; incorporates holistic, naturopathic practices; and has elevation changes from 200 to 1000 ft

Facts: Established 2001 (planted 1997) • 538 acres (about half of that producing, all in McMinnville AVA) • 13,000 cases annually

Owners: Moe and Flora Momtazi
Winemaker: Tahmiene Momtazi

Date visited: _____

Went with: _____

Notes: _____

_____

by Ron Kaplan

Panther Creek

● ●

www.panthercreekcellars.com
455 NE Irvine; McMinnville; 503.472.8080

Hours: Daily 12:00pm–5:00pm (year-round)

Tasting Fee: $5.00 Flight of 5 tastings

Wine: 7–8 varieties; $20.00-$60.00
Specializes in Pinot Noir

Notes: Formerly the Public Power Works of McMinnville, this historic building found a new calling as the Panther Creek Winery. The super-high, steel-beamed ceilings and dark, rust-painted brick walls around the tasting area give it an industrial feel, but the unique wood bar and furnishings make it a very warm and cool-looking space. Plop yourself down at the big group seating table, or if you're ready for a picnic, head to the garden area out back. • Winery originally founded by Ken Wright, and sold in 1993. Current tasting room opened in 2006.

Facts: Established 1986 • Sources grapes throughout the Willamette Valley • 7,500 cases annually

Owner: Liz Chambers
Winemaker: Michael Stevenson

Date visited: _____
Went with: _____
Notes: _____
_____

Photos by John Valls

decor

food for sale

event space

gift shop

R. Stuart & Co. Wine Bar

• •

www.rstuartandco.com
528 NE Third Street; McMinnville; 503.472.4477

Hours: Wed–Sat 12:00pm–7:00pm (8:00pm Fri–Sat
Spring–Fall) and Sunday 12:00pm–5:00pm

Tasting Fee: $10.00 White Flight of 3 tastings;
$12.00 Flight of 3 Pinot Noirs
Specializes in Pinot Noir

Wine: 12 varieties (R. Stuart and Big Fire brands);
$10.00–$50.00; Specializes in Pinot Noir

Notes: This downtown McMinnville, French-style
café/wine bar throws down the full array of cute-
ness including white lace curtains, creamy yellow
walls, wood floors and antique-style chandeliers. The
back bar glows and beckons with bright, shiny wine
glasses and has giant-sized wine bottles for added
appeal. There's a big group table with several romantic
two-tops. The actual winemaking facilities are just
a few blocks away in an old granary converted to
a winery.

Facts: Established 2001 • Sources grapes from all
over Oregon • 22,000 cases annually

Owners: Rob and Maria Stuart
Winemaker: Rob Stuart

Date visited: _____

Went with: _____

Notes: _____

_____

by Lenny Breedbate

WineWorks Oregon

● ●

www.walnutcitywineworks.com
475 NE 17th Street; McMinnville; 503.472.3215

Hours: Thurs–Sun 11:00am–4:30pm (year-round)

Tasting Fee: $5.00 flight of 6-7 tastes

Wine: 25 varieties (four different wine labels);
$20.00–$60.00
Specializes in Pinot Noir and boutique whites

Notes: A group of vintners who share a passion for
Pinot Noir and fair value in the marketplace produce
premium wines in this urban winery in the heart of
McMinnville. • Inside, you'll take a step back in time
with fabulous flea market finds and good wines.
Vintage travel posters adorn the muted aqua walls
and the low lighting and dark tiled bar adds appeal.

Facts: Established 2000 • All together manage
300 acres • Willamette Valley AVAs • 18,000 cases
annually total

Winemakers:
Walnut City Wineworks: John Gilpin and John Davidson
Z'IVO: John and Kathy Zelko
Bernard Machado: John Davidson
Robinson Reserve: Miguel Lopez and John Davidson

Date visited: _____
Went with: _____
Notes: _____

view

fanciness

deck/patio

food for sale

picnic area

bus/rv

pet friendly

tours

event space

Yamhill Valley

www.yamhill.com
16250 S.W. Oldsville Road; McMinnville; 503.843.3100

Hours: Daily 11:00am–5:00pm (summer);
Sat–Sun 11:00am–5:00pm (Sep–May, closed Jan–Feb)

Tasting Fee: $5.00 flight of 5 tastes

Wine: 8 varieties; $12.00-$35.00
Specializes in Pinot Noir

Outside: Nice and nestled deep and away from the highway with a koi pond (fish food for sale). Head to the big, back deck for a spectacular view of the coastal range, or hang out front for fab views while picnicking.

Inside: Simple interior with sky-high windows, tiled floors and wood beams. Antique cupboards, tapestries and dried floral arrangements lend country charm.

Notes: As one of the first vineyards in the area, it got dibs in early for getting to name the wine after the county. • All in the family and family-friendly.

Facts: Established 1983 • 150 acres (100 planted)
• McMinnville AVA • 17,000 cases annually

Owners: Denis Burger, Elaine McCall, and David and Terri Hinrichs
Winemaker: Stephen Cary

Date visited: _____
Went with: _____
Notes: _____
_____

Youngberg Hill

www.youngberghill.com
10660 SW Youngberg Hill Road; McMinnville;
503.472.2727

Hours: Mon–Fri 11:00am–5:00pm (year-round))

Tasting Fee: $5.00 for 4-5 tastes

Wine: 4-5 varieties; $18.00-$50.00
Specializes in Pinot Noir

Outside: This exquisite winery estate and B&B is a prominent stand-out way up high on Youngberg Hill. Surrounded by grape vines and remarkable floral landscaping with views of Mt. Hood, the Cascades, Jefferson and the Sisters. Gorgeous!!

Inside: This eight-room historic inn has a game room, library and a beautiful wine room with an adjacent balcony. This romantic spot is one not to be missed!

Notes: Named after the original farm that the vineyard now resides on. • Organic, LIVE and Salmon-Safe.
• Incredible outdoor venue for a beautiful winery wedding and officially one of the best places to kiss.

Facts: Established1989 • 50 acres • McMinnville AVA
• 1,500 cases annually

Owner: Wayne Bailey
Winemaker: Wayne Bailey

Date visited: _____
Went with: _____
Notes: _____
_____

Approx. 10 miles

Listed in
McMinnville
Section

Yamhill
Valley

Maysara

Muddy Valley

Oldsville

18

Amity

Kri
Hill

Amity

Coelho

5th

Bellevue

Rice Lane

Mia Sona

Amity/Nurse

Bellevue

99

Broadmead

Ballston

Bethel

Bethel

Oak Grove

Namasté

Sunnyside

Van Well

99

Left Coast

Cher
Hill

Crowley

Perrydale

Starr

Van Duzer

Smithfield

Farmer

Chataeu
Bianca

22

Firesteed

Eola
Hills

Eola/Amity — East Side

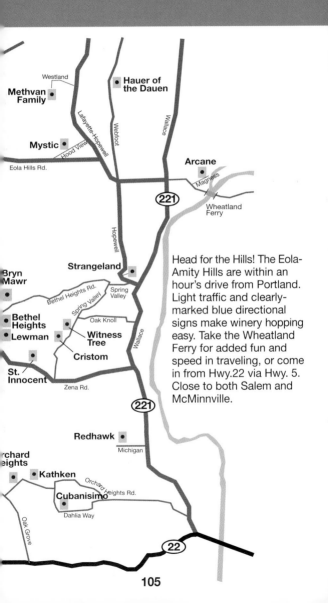

Methvan Family

Westland

Hauer of the Dauen

Lafayette-Hopewell

Webfoot

Wallace

Mystic

Hood View

Eola Hills Rd.

Arcane

Magness

221

Wheatland Ferry

Hopewell

Bryn Mawr

Strangeland

Bethel Heights Rd.

Spring Valley

Spring Valley

Bethel Heights

Lewman

Oak Knoll

Witness Tree

Wallace

Cristom

St. Innocent

Zena Rd.

Head for the Hills! The Eola-Amity Hills are within an hour's drive from Portland. Light traffic and clearly-marked blue directional signs make winery hopping easy. Take the Wheatland Ferry for added fun and speed in traveling, or come in from Hwy.22 via Hwy. 5. Close to both Salem and McMinnville.

Redhawk

Michigan

221

Orchard Heights

Kathken

Orchard Heights Rd.

Cubanisimo

Dahlia Way

Oak Grove

22

view

fanciness

deck/patio

food for sale

picnic area

bus/rv

pet friendly

tours

event space

Amity Vineyards
• •

www.amityvineyards.com
18150 SE Amity Vineyards Road; Amity; 503.835.2362

Hours: Daily 11:00am–6:00pm (Jun–Sep);
Daily 12:00pm–5:00pm (Oct–May)

Tasting Fee: $5.00 flight of 6+ tastes

Wine: 12-15 varieties; $15.00–$39.00
Specializes in Pinot Noir, Germanic Whites, organic

Outside: The views from the big red barn winery go
on forever! This is a perfect place for a picnic.

Inside: The tasting room is in the front end of the
winery and seems to incorporate some of its history.
The bar top showcases a myriad of old labels. They
have a small giftshop area too.

Notes: One of Oregon's oldest wineries and early
pioneers in establishing an impressive reputation for
Oregon Pinot Noirs. • "Amity" means friendship and is
also the name of the AVA and town. • LIVE certified.

Facts: Established 1974 • 80 acres (15 in production) • Eola Hills/Amity AVA, plus grapes from other
"green" Willamette Valley Vineyards • 12,000 cases

Owner: Myron Redford
Winemaker: Darcy Pendergrass

Date visited: _____
Went with: _____
Notes: _____
_____

Arcane Cellars

• •

www.arcanecellars.com
22350 Magness Road; Wheatland; 503.868.7076

Hours: Sat-Sun 12:00pm–4:00pm (year-round)

Tasting Fee: $5.00 Flight of 6+

Wine: 9 varieties; $16.00-$24.00
Specializes in Pinot Gris and Pinot Gris Rosé

Outside: Just down river and around the corner from the Wheatland Ferry, the Arcane Cellars is uniquely situated along the Willamette River. Orchards and vineyards surround the winery, inviting you to take a walk around. Or just sit on the deck or picnic riverside.

Inside: The mobile tasting bar will be found outside on nice days or in the production area on not-so-nice days. It's nicer outside!

Notes: The mesmerizing symbols found on the labels would be recognizable to your local alchemist or magician as that of gold or silver.

Facts: Established 2002 • 30 acres (16 planted) • Willamette Valley AVA, plus grapes from other AVAs throughout Oregon • 3,500 cases annually

Owner: Jason Silva
Winemaker: Jason Silva

Date visited: _____
Went with: _____
Notes: _____
_____

view

fanciness

deck/patio

food for sale

picnic area

bus/rv

pet friendly

tours

event space

Bethel Heights

. . . .

www.bethelheights.com
6060 Bethel Heights Road; Salem; 503.581.2262

Hours: Tues–Sun 11:00am-5:00pm (May–Oct);
Sat–Sun 11:00am-5:00pm (Mar, Apr, and Nov)
Closed Dec–Feb

Tasting Fee: $5.00 flight of 6 tastes

Wine: 12 varieties; $18.00-$50.00
Specializes in Pinot Noir

Outside: A minister from Bethel called it "The Heights
of Bethel" and it *is* heavenly! Gorgeous views from high
atop a bluff with a panoramic view of vineyards, valleys
and distant mountains, including Mt. Jefferson.

Inside: Two walls of windows converge to frame the
outside from the inside. Simple, modern, chalet style.

Notes: • Directly across the road is the Bethel
Heights Farm Bed & Breakfast (503.364.7688)

Facts: Established 1984 (1977 plantings) • 70 acres
• Eola-Amity Hills AVA; 15% other Willamette Valley
AVAs • 12,000 cases annually

Owners: Terry Casteel, Marilyn Webb, Ted Casteel,
Pat Dudley and Barbara Dudley
Winemakers: Terry Casteel, Ben Casteel

Date visited: _____
Went with: _____
Notes: _____
_____

Bryn Mawr

• •

www.brynmawrvineyards.com
5955 Bethel Heights Road NW; Salem; 503.581.4286

Hours: Sat-Sun 11:00am-5:00pm (year round)

Tasting Fee: $5.00 flight of 4-6 tastes

Wine: 7 varieties; $25.00-$45.00
Specializes in Pinot Noir

Outside: Forget the Jones'... keeping up with the
Lloyd-Jones' would be a better plan. The front yard
is a vineyard, the back yard has a spectacular view
of the coastal range, and best part is that the house
is also a winery! Plus, there are sheep that mow the
grass!

Inside: The basement of the house serves as the
winery and tasting room, super-bare-bones simple.

Notes: It's easy to see why they call this Bryn Mawr;
it means "high hill" in Welsh. There's also added
meaning and philosophy behind those words.

Facts: Established 2002 (1994 first plantings)
• 15 acres (4 planted) • Eola-Amity Hills AVA
• 500 cases annually

Owner: David Lloyd-Jones
Winemaker: David Lloyd-Jones

Date visited: _____
Went with: _____
Notes: _____

view

fanciness

deck/patio

food for sale

picnic area

bus/rv

pet friendly

tours

event space

Chateau Bianca

● ●

www.chateaubianca.com
17485 Highway 22; Dallas; 503.623.6181

Hours: Daily 10:00am-5:00pm (year-round)

Tasting Fee: $5.00 per flight of 6 tastes (red or white)

Wine: 20 varieties; $12.00-$30.00
Specializes in "Gluhwein" (unique German-style)

Outside: Right off the highway, it's a bit loud, but still nice for a picnic with expansive views of open fields.

Inside: Country German charm with a big wine-related gift shop provides a fun environment to sip and shop. Very friendly here with some good "beginner" wines.

Notes: Sweet retreat B&B on property, and owners Helmut and Liselotte Wetzel speak both German and English. • Bianca is their daughter and namesake of the winery. • Don't miss sampling the Gluhwine!

Facts: Established 1990 • 100 acres (50 planted)
• Willamette Valley AVA • 12,000 cases annually

Owner: Helmut Wetzel
Winemaker: Helmut Wetzel

Date visited: _____
Went with: _____
Notes: _____
_____

ew

siness

/patio

for sale

c area

s/rv

riendly

ours

space

Cherry Hill

• •

www.cherryhillwinery.com
7867 Crowley Road, Rickreall; 503.623.7867

Hours: Sat–Sun 11:00am-5:00pm; call weekdays
11:00am–4:00pm (May 1–Oct 1); and by appt.

Tasting Fee: $10.00 for 5 tastes

Wine: 7 varieties; $16.00-$29.00
Specializes in Pinot Noir

Outside: The long drive up the gravel road gives you
pretty, expansive views of undulating, vine-covered
hills and valleys. Continue past the super-cute guest
cottages (occasionally available only with wine club
membership and two case purchase – inquire within).

Inside: Share a toast with Diogenes, the Greek wine
philosopher painted on the wall (who also bears a
slight likeness to the owner). Woody, with a piano too!

Notes: Each label is different – don't miss Papillon
Pinot with Miss Daisy, the dog who drinks wine and
has wine-glass-shaped fur! • Cherry Hill name comes
from the original cherry orchard on the property.

Facts: Established 2003 • 100 acres (88 planted)
• Eola-Amity Hills AVA • 4,000 cases annually

Owners: Mike and Jan Sweeney
Winemaker: Chris Luby

Date visited: _____
Went with: _____
Notes: _____
_____

decor

food for sale

event space

gift shop

Coelho Winery
• •

www.coelhowinery.com
111 5th Street; Amity; 503.835.9305

Hours: Daily 11:00am–5:00pm (Apr–mid-Dec);
Fri–Sun 11:00am–5:00pm (Jan–Mar)

Tasting Fee: $5.00 flight of 4 tastes;
$7.00 for 2 Ports plus chocolate pairings

Wine: 16 varieties; $16.00–35.00
Specializes in Pinot Noir, Pinot Gris, Chardonnay
and Portuguese-style varietals

Notes: You wouldn't really guess it from the exterior,
but inside you'll find a welcoming and well-designed
space full of warmth and charm. There's a showpiece
living room seating area with comfy couches, oriental
rug and a giant brick fireplace. Heavy woods salvaged
from an old granary give substance and character to
furnishings. • Coelho (Co-EL-ho) is the owners' last
name which means rabbit in Portuguese (an abstract
rabbit logo is on every label, along with a Portuguese
translation of a positive word like "paciencia" meaning
patience. Big event room for lunch or weddings.

Facts: Established 2005 • 30 acres • Eola-Amity Hills
AVA, plus Portuguese varietal grapes • 3,000 cases

Owners: Dave and Deolinda Coelho
Winemaker: Brian Marcy

Date visited: _____
Went with: _____
Notes: _____

ew

iness

/patio

for sale

c area

s/rv

riendly

urs

space

Cristom

●●●●●●●●●●●●●●●●●●●●●●●●●●●●●●

www.cristomwines.com
6905 Spring Valley Road NW; Salem; 503.375.3068

Hours: Tues–Sun 11:00am–5:00pm (Apr–Nov);
Open by appointment (Dec–Mar)

Tasting Fee: $5.00 flight of 6 tastes

Wine: 10 varieties; $20.00–50.00
Specializes in Pinot Noir

Outside: An Eola Hills stand-out with some nice
amenities thrown in: brick sidewalks made for strolling,
beautifully landscaped grounds, lots of picnic tables,
garden benches, and even a view of Mt. Jefferson.

Inside: Old-world style greets you at the entrance
with massive 250-year-old mahogany doors from
France. Provencal charm continues inside with high
wood-beamed ceilings, antique globe chandeliers,
tiled terra-cotta floors and mottled golden walls.

Notes: Named for the Gerrie children, Chris and Tom.
• The eight vineyards are all named in honor of family
matriarchs (the "ladies").

Facts: Established 1994 • 120 acres (65 planted)
• Eola-Amity Hills AVA • 10,000 cases annually

Owners: Paul and Eileen Gerrie
Winemaker: Steve Doerner

Date visited: _____
Went with: _____
Notes: _____

view

fanciness

deck/patio

food for sale

picnic area

bus/rv

pet friendly

tours

event space

Cubanisimo

● ●

www.cubanisimovineyards.com
1754 Best Road NW; Salem; 503.588.1763

Hours: Daily 11:00am–5:00pm (Apr–Dec);
Closed mid-Dec–Mar

Tasting Fee: $5.00 flight of 5-6 tastings

Wine: 7 varieties; $15.00–29.00
Specializes in Pinot Noir

Outside: Take a tropical vacation of the mind and
enjoy the wonderful, lushly landscaped wine garden
out back. Kick back and relax on the grande patio.

Inside: Refined, slight Cuban look without excessive
color. Lots of barrel-tasting tables, banana-leaf ceiling
fans, some nice posters and prints, with a few gifts too.

Notes: Take salsa lessons year-round on every third
Saturday. • Named in honor of owner's Cuban heritage,
hailing from Havana. Hunt for Cuban effects throughout. • No winery on site (bottled at R.Stuart).

Facts: Established 2003 (vineyard since 1991) • 21
acres (12 planted) • Eola-Amity Hills AVA • 1,500 cases

Owner: Mauricio Collada, Jr.
Winemaker: Robert Stuart

Date visited: _____
Went with: _____
Notes: _____

Eola Hills Wine Cellars

• •

www.eolahillswinery.com
501 South Pacific Hwy 99; Rickreall; 503.623.2405

Hours: Daily 10:00am–5:00pm (year-round)

Tasting Fee: FREE flight of 6+ tastes

Wine: 25 varieties; $7.00–$25.00
Specializes in a large array of wine styles!

Outside: Positioned right off Hwy. 99 with koi pond and man-made waterfall to help you immediately forget traffic. Around back there's a large patio under a portico and big lawn with several picnic tables.

Inside: Eola Hills Wine Cellars is a versatile facility with a gift shop, event area and tasting room, all blended together with a raw, country-store feel. They bring the outside in with a garden arbor over the huge, three-sided, copper-top tasting bar that makes for a popular social scene. Event space up to 300.

Notes: The name Eola is derived from Aeolus, the Greek God of wind. • Don't miss the Sunday Brunch if you're in the area! • Bike Oregon Sundays in August.

Facts: Established 1986 (1981 plantings) • 300 acres (30 planted in Eola-Amity Hills) • 60,000 cases annually

Owner: Tom Huggins
Winemaker: Steve Anderson

Date visited: _____

Went with: _____

Notes: _____

_____

view

fanciness

deck/patio

food for sale

picnic area

bus/rv

pet friendly

tours

event space

Firesteed
•••••••••••••••••••••••••••••

www.firesteed.com
2200 N. Pacific Hwy (99W); Rickreall; 503.623.8683

Hours: Daily 11:00am–5:00pm (year-round)

Tasting Fee: FREE flight of 6+ tastes

Wine: 25 varieties; $7.00–$25.00
Specializes in having a large array of wine styles

Outside: Fields go on forever in every direction here, and it just seems like a place where a powerful horse would love to run wild. Picnic patio is badly positioned near driveway and barn that blocks the view.

Inside: It's a brand-spankin' new tasting room that warms things up from a cold metal exterior. Nice space, but no viewing windows of the view outside. It's all about focusing on the wine (and wine being made).

Notes: The name Firesteed derives very loosely from the owner's last name meaning Horse Brook, but "fire" was more exciting than water/brook, and a "steed" is not just a horse. • Other delicious wines are tasted here as well: Flynn, Citation and Cayalla.

Facts: Established 1992 (1982 plantings) • 200 acres (plus other WA and OR sources) • 85,000 cases annually

Owner: Howard Rossbach
Winemaker: Bryan Croft

Date visited: _____
Went with: _____
Notes: _____
_____

Hauer of the Dauen

• •

(no website)
16425 SE Webfoot Road; Dayton; 503.868.7359

Hours: Sat–Sun 12:00pm–5:00pm (closed Xmas–Jan)

Tasting Fee: FREE flight of 6+ tastes; $4.00 groups;
$10.00 fee if you are grumpy or irritable!

Wine: 14 varieties; $10.00–$16.00
Specializes in drinkable, value wines; Only ones in
Oregon that do Lemberger; also Gamay Noir

Outside: Located out in the flatland farmlands, it
makes for a great bike trip and picnic destination.

Inside: Not at all too fancy (barrels, cement floors,
white plastic table and chairs, etc.), but with Carl
behind the bar, you'll have great company!

Notes: They "like to approach things a little differently"
here, and the end result is a wide array of affordable
wines served up with wise words and humor. • The
name Dauenhauer means striking of the sunrise.
• The owner/winemaker is a beloved local character!

Facts: Established 1998 (1980 plantings) • 140 acres
Willamette Valley AVA (they sell grapes to others)
• 4,000 cases average annually

Owner: Carl Dauenhauer
Winemaker: Carl Dauenhauer

Date visited: _____
Went with: _____
Notes: _____
_____

117

view

fanciness

deck/patio

food for sale

picnic area

bus/rv

pet friendly

tours

event space

Kathken

• •

www.kathkenvineyards.com
5739 Orchard Heights Road; Salem; 503.316.3911

Hours: Sat–Sun 12:00pm–5:00pm (summer)

Tasting Fee: $1.00 per taste (make your own flight);
$5.00 for full flight

Wine: 10 varieties; $14.00-$25.00
Specializes in Pinor Noir and Pinot Gris

Outside: Low-key and very casual place currently
positioned at the bottom of a big vineyard hill, but
they are moving on up to a deluxe yurt in the sky!
There's also a fun party area in a grove of trees with
giant branches protecting a big group of picnic tables.
Weekend concert nights are a blast all summer long.

Inside: Spruced-up, open-air garage serves as curren
tasting room. The yurt on the hill will be done soon and
offer beautiful views of the fields below and away!

Notes: Live bands every weekend all summer long.
• Lots of room to roam and run. Good hiking.

Facts: Established 2000 • 51 acres (40 producing)
• Eola-Amity Hills AVA • 2,000 cases annually

Owners: Ken and Kathy Slusser
Winemaker: Ken Slusser

Date visited: _____
Went with: _____
Notes: _____
_____

ew

iness

/patio

or sale

c area

s/rv

iendly

urs

space

Kristin Hill

• •

(no website)
3330 SE Amity-Dayton Hwy: Amity; 503.835.0850

Hours: Daily 12:00pm–5:00pm (Mar–Dec);
Sat-Sun 12:00pm-5:00pm (Jan–Feb)

Tasting Fee: FREE flight of 4-5 tastes

Wine: 12 varieties; $12.00–$25.00
Specializes in Sparkling Wines, Nouveau, Port

Outside: Just north of Amity you'll find this small
German style "Weinstube Haus" next door to a few
giant fir trees and a flower-lined path. There's a cozy
deck with a couple of tables where you can enjoy a
glass with friends and enjoy the view.

Inside: An old-school, German Weinstube (a Wine
Tasting Room) theme where flowers, wood beams and
lace decorate the "living" room. Reach-thru tasting bar.

Notes: Named after the Aberg's daughter, Kristin.
• Overall, the tasting room is more on the rustic side
with authentic farm-country style.

Facts: Established 1990 • 34 acres (24 producing
Eola-Amity Hills AVA) • 2,200 cases annually

Owners: Eric and Linda Aberg
Winemaker: Eric Aberg

Date visited: _____
Went with: _____
Notes: _____
_____

view

fanciness

deck/patio

food for sale

picnic area

bus/rv

pet friendly

tours

event space

Left Coast Cellars

• •

www.leftcoastcellars.com
4225 N Pacific Hwy (99W); Rickreall; 888.831.4916

Hours: Daily 12:00pm–5:00pm (Feb–Dec);
by appointment only Christmas thru January

Tasting Fee: $5.00 flight of 5-6 tastes

Wine: 10 varieties; $15.00–$60.00
Specializes in Pinot Noir

Outside: Winding roads and a pretty drive take you
past a pond and through the vineyards, and just a
few more left turns and you finally arrive at the tasting
room. The nearby, old growth oak grove has plenty of
room for a picnic in the grass or on the covered patio.

Inside: The refurbished tasting room has a warm,
open feel with wood floors, lots of windows, and
modern twists on appealing country-style decor.

Notes: Named for the abundance of lefties in the
Pfaff family. But do be sure to pick-up a few Left
Coast souvenirs for your Republican friends! They
are conservative however, in that they get as much
as 60% of their electricity from solar panels.

Facts: Established 2003 • 300 acres (100 producing)
Willamette Valley AVA • 4,500 cases annually

Owners: Suzanne Pfaff and family
Winemaker: Luke McCollom

Date visited: _____
Went with: _____
Notes: _____
_____

Lewman

• •

www.lewmanvineyard.com
6080 Bethel Heights Road; Salem; 503.365.8859

Hours: Sat–Sun 11:00am–5:00pm (Mar–Oct);
by appointment only off season; closed Dec–Feb

Tasting Fee: $1.00 per taste

Wine: 3 varieties; $25.00–$35.00
Specializes in Pinot Noir

Outside: Take a trip to experience the simple life
out in the farmlands. Tasting room is inside owners'
country home with back relaxation or party deck
possibly available. Sustainably managed farming.

Inside: Simple, remodeled sun porch turned tasting
room has big viewing windows all around. Small
place (only 300 cases) with big hearts and wines.

Notes: Kaoru is Japanese and you will see her influence
on the website and in its photo gallery.

Facts: Established 2002 (1992 plantings) • 17 acres
(6.5 planted); Eola-Amity Hills AVA • 300 cases

Owners: Dennis and Kaoru Lewman
Winemaker: Dennis Lewman

Date visited: _____
Went with: _____
Notes: _____
_____

view

fanciness

deck/patio

food for sale

picnic area

bus/rv

romance factor

tours

event space

Methven Family Vineyards

www.methvenfamilyvineyards.com
11400 Westland Lane; Dayton; 503.868.7259

Hours: Wed-Sun 11:00am–5:00pm (wine season);
Fri-Sun 11:00am–5:00pm (winter)

Tasting Fee: $5.00 flight of 5 tastes

Wine: 6 varieties; $15.00–$28.00
Specializes in Pinot Noir (going to all estate wines)

Outside: The long and winding road takes you around
and through the vineyards to the all-new and impressive
tasting room. On a clear day you can see Mt. Hood,
Mt. Jefferson *and* Mt. Adams! Great views from the
tasting bar, patio area and/or bocce ball court.

Inside: Rehab has never looked better! Big, open,
and spacious room, anchored in gorgeous deep
woods. The bar itself is a giant slab of rough-hewn,
heavily lacquered maple atop a rocky base. The custom-
made cherry wood wall unit cabinetwork demands
appreciation. Cheese and crackers are served on
an over-sized, elegant wooden dinner table.

Facts: Established 2004 • 100 acres (30 planted)
• Eola-Amity Hills AVA • 4,000 cases annually

Owners: Allen and Jill Methven
Winemaker: Chris Lubberstedt

Date visited: _____
Went with: _____
Notes: _____
_____

decor

for sale

space

shop

Mia Sonatina Cellars
● ●

www.miasonatina.com
102 Nursery Street; Amity; 503.449.0834

Hours: Fri-Sun 11:00am–5:00pm (Feb–Dec);
By appointment only (Jan)

Tasting Fee: FREE flight of 6+ tastes

Wine: 12 varieties; $10.00–$25.00
Specializes in unique, old-world style

Notes: From the street, this winery building appears as any big ol' white warehouse, but there's magic playing behind those giant wood doors! Inside, the tasting room is attached to the winery so it's pretty cold, but both the hosts and Italian villa decor warm things up. • An illuminated, hand-crafted display showcase is big enough for many more awards to come. • Mia Sonatina means "My Little Song" in Italian and can be taken to mean a song for the palate.

Facts: Established 2003 • Sources grapes from variety of Oregon AVAs • 1,200 cases annually

Owners: Jo and Vern Spencer
Winemaker: Vern Spencer

Date visited: _____
Went with: _____
Notes: _____
_____

view

fanciness

deck/patio

food for sale

picnic area

bus/rv

pet friendly

tours

event space

Mystic

●●●●●●●●●●●●●●●●●●●●●●●●●●

www.mysticwine.com
3995 Deepwood Lane NW; Salem; 503.581.2769

Hours: Sat–Sun 12:00pm–5:00pm (closed Dec–Feb)

Tasting Fee: $5.00; flight of 5-6 tastes

Wine: 6-8 varieties; $20.00–$28.00
Specializes in "Noble Northwest Reds"

Outside: You can see pretty much the full line-up
of mountains here! At the winery, this well-designed
labor-of-love is energy efficient inside-out from
salvaged hop-kiln doors to 12" thick insulation.

Inside: The current tasting room is inside the house
when you first drive up. It has a cozy, ski-lodge feel
with a sunken living room and fireplace.

Notes: The award-winning label uses art drawn by
Rick's son Dillon—something he did when he was
only 11 years old. • Divine Providence and a Mythical
Merlot led to the Mystic name (too awkward to say
"mythical" sometimes when drinking).

Facts: Established 1992 • 10 acres in Eola-Amity
Hills AVA (plus grapes from Columbia Gorge AVA)
• 2,000 cases annually

Owner: Rick Mafit
Winemaker: Rick Mafit

Date visited: _____

Went with: _____

Notes: _____

_____

Namasté

• •

www.namastevineyards.com
5600 Van Well Road; Dallas; 503.623.4150

Hours: Sat–Sun 12:00pm–6:00pm (closed Jan–Feb)

Tasting Fee: $5.00 flight of 6+ tastes

Wine: 8 varieties; $12.00–$34.00
Specializes in Estate Pinot Noir

Outside: The peaceful journey begins with a nice
country drive out to the serenity of Namasté Vineyards. You can't tell from its outer appearance, but
this is a revamped Q-hut. Nice views and breezes.

Inside: You are welcomed inside this arched, golden,
honeycomb room with the Namasté logo proclaiming:
"The spirit of the wine honors the spirit of the vine."
Very simple and pleasant interior with extra-long bar.

Notes: What do you get when a master carpenter,
a computer guy and a new age life coach want to
combine forces with their love of wine and Eastern
philosophies? Namasté Vineyards and wine names
like Peace, Serenity, Prosperity and Abundance!

Facts: Established 2003 (1980 plantings) • 32 acres
• Willamette Valley AVA • 4,000 cases annually

Owners: Dave Masciorini; Sonia and Chris Miller
Winemaker: Andreas Wetzel

Date visited: _____
Went with: _____
Notes: _____
_____

view

fanciness

deck/patio

food for sale

picnic area

bus/rv

pet friendly

tours

event space

Orchard Heights Winery

www.orchardheightswinery.com
6057 Orchard Heights Winery; Salem; 503.391.7308

Hours: Daily 11:00am–5:00pm (year-round);
Sunday Brunch 9:00am–1:00pm

Tasting Fee: $1.00 per red; $.50 per white

Wine: 20 varieties; $8.00-$25.00
Specializes in variety and sweet-style wines

Outside: There are a couple of exceptionally outstanding places to sit out and enjoy stunning views. Choose from the wonderful back deck with a pool or front gazebo with garden arbor and chairs.

Inside: There's a huge gift shop here with tons of fun items and lots of sweet treats (the owners also have a chocolate factory in Hawaii). You can get lunch here—sit back and enjoy their charming, country style with stellar views through the giant windows.

Notes: Big-time wedding capabilities with room for up to 400 guests. • Hawaiian influences with an array of 5 "tropical" wines like pineapple or mango.

Facts: Established 1996 (1960's plantings) • 15 acres (2.5 planted) • Eola-Amity Hills • 20,000 cases annually

Owners: Gwen and Micheal Purdy
Winemaker: Carole Wyscaver

Date visited: _____
Went with: _____
Notes: _____
_____

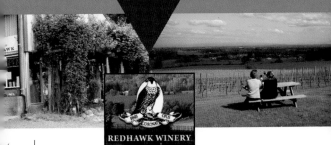

Redhawk Winery

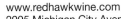

www.redhawkwine.com
2995 Michigan City Avenue NW; Salem; 503.362.1596

Hours: Daily 11:00am–5:00pm (year-round)

Tasting Fee: $5.00 flight of 6+ tastes

Wine: 8-12 varieties; $11.00–$30.00
Specializes in the infamous Grateful Red Pinot Noir

Outside: Spectacular 180° view of the entire Eastern mountain range including our beloved Mt. Hood. There's a second picnic haven with several tables and a treehouse under a grove of soaring pines.

Inside: Yes! This renovated tasting room has wall-to-wall-to-ceiling windows which allow you to absorb the hugely expansive, beautiful view laid out before you.

Notes: Named for the Red-tailed hawks that circle around the area. • Redhawk Winery was founded in 1988, then purchased and overhauled in 2005.

Facts: Established 2005 (1978 plantings) • 23 acres (15 planted) • Eola-Amity AVA • 4,200 cases annually

Owners: John and Betty Pataccoli
Winemaker: John Pataccoli

Date visited: _____

Went with: _____

Notes: _____

_____

view

fanciness

deck/patio

food for sale

picnic area

bus/rv

pet friendly

tours

event space

St. Innocent

www.stinnocentwine.com
5657 Zena Road; Salem; 503.378.1526

Hours: Tues–Sun 11:00am-5:00pm (May–Oct);
Fri–Sun 11:00am–4:00pm (Nov–Apr)

Tasting Fee: $5.00 Flight of 7

Wine: 10 varieties; $20.00-$39.00
Specializes in signature Sparklings and Pinot Noir

Outside: This European, storybook gatehouse is a standout in the farmlands amoungst its country cousins. As you drive past the large fountain and up to the entryway, the Zenith Vineyard stretches up the hill to the west. A very memorable and romantic place.

Inside: The tasting room in the west wing is done up in a modern, country-kitchen style with plenty of room and lots of light. Plus 17,500 sq. ft Zenith Event Center.

Notes: Owner's father was born on All Innocents Day and his middle name is "Innocent.". • They produce seven single vineyard Pinot Noirs. • $5.00 group tours.

Facts: Established 1988 • 133 acres (80 planted in Zenith Vineyard plus Willamette Valley AVA grapes) • 9,000 cases annually

Owner: Mark Vlossak
Winemaker: Mark Vlossak

Date visited: _____

Went with: _____

Notes: _____

_____

iew

ciness

/patio

for sale

ic area

us/rv

friendly

ours

t space

Stangeland

www.stangelandwinery.com
8500 Hopewell Road; Salem; 503.581.0355

Hours: Wed–Sun 12:00pm-5:00pm (summer);
Sat–Sun 12:00pm–5:00pm (off-season)

Tasting Fee: $5.00 for 6+ tastes

Wine: 19 varieties; $10.00-$35.00
Specializes in Pinot Noir and Pinot Gris

Outside: Inside and out, Stangeland portrays a
strong "Northwest-Nordic-Tuscan" style with huge
wooden doors, stone walls and the requisite party
patio positioned for the great views down the valley.

Inside: The tasting bar is set up right inside this small
winery, and fits right in with the wine barrels. Arches,
thick rugs, and textured gold walls are nice touches.

Notes: Stangeland Winery gets its name from an
area in Norway. Look closely—it's *not* Strangeland.
• Study hard and impress the lads here with your
Norwegian toasts ("Skål!" [pronounced skole].)

Facts: Established 1992 (first plantings 1978)
• 4.5 acres on-site in Eola-Amity Hills AVA (plus
sourced nearby grapes) • 2,600 cases

Owner: Larry D. Miller
Winemaker: Larrry D. Miller

Date visited: _____
Went with: _____
Notes: _____
_____

view

fanciness

deck/patio

food for sale

picnic area

bus/rv

pet friendly

tours

event space

Van Duzer

• •

www.vanduzer.com
11075 Smithfield Road; Dallas; 800.884.1927

Hours: Daily 11:00am–5:00pm; Closed Jan–Feb

Tasting Fee: $10.00 for 5 tastes

Wine: 11 varieties; $11.00-$52.00;
Specializes in Pinot Noir and Pinot Gris

Outside: Gorgeous facility and oh, yeah, stellar views too! Set on the west side of a hill facing the coastal range with a large stone patio facing south, you'll enjoy expansive views in almost every direction.

Inside: Award-winning decor in modern art nouveau style with a touch of whimsy. The gorgeous interior reflects artwork touches found on the Van Duzer Vineyards wine labels. Bring your designer friends!

Notes: Named for its proximity to east end of the Van Duzer corridor. • 100% of the Van Duzer line-up is estate wine. • The vineyard is Salmon-Safe and LIVE certified. Set an appointment for you and your friends to sit at the VIP tasting table.

Facts: Established 1998 • 140 acres (82 planted)
• Willamette Valley AVA • 18,000 cases annually

Owners: Carl and Marilyn Thoma
Winemaker: Jim Kakacek

Date visited: _____
Went with: _____
Notes: _____
_____

Witness Tree

•••••••••••••••••••••••••••••

www.witnesstreevineyard.com
7111 Spring Valley Road NW; Salem; 503.585.7874

Hours: Tues–Sun 11:00am–5:00pm (May–Oct);
Sat–Sun 11:00am–5:00pm (Nov–Apr)

Tasting Fee: $10.00 Flight of 6 tastes

Wine: 11 varieties; $14.00–$48.00
Specializes in Pinot Noir

Outside: Picnic on the open grassy knoll next to the
vineyard—with views of Mt. Hood and Mt. Jefferson
too! Or simply sit n' sip on the white, wooden front
porch and quickly kick into relaxation mode.

Inside: Welcome to the country life and a small,
simple living-room-style tasting room with basic white
walls and just a few wicker chairs.

Notes: The vineyard takes its name from an ancient
oak tree used as a surveyor's landmark in 1854. The
tree still stands as an official Oregon State "Heritage
Tree" and has a beautiful and strong presence over
the vineyard. • LIVE and Salmon-Safe certified.

Facts: Established 1986 •100 acres (half producing
in Eola-Amity Hills AVA) • 6,000 cases annually

Owners: Carolyn and Dennis Devine
Winemaker: Steven Westby

Date visited: _____
Went with: _____
Notes: _____
_____

Here's the south side of the Willamette Valley. Please note the mileage scale. This area is more spread out in comparison to other maps. Roads are more winding than they appear!

iew

ciness

k/patio

for sale

ic area

us/rv

friendly

ours

nt space

Airlie

• •

www.airliewinery.com
15305 Dunn Forest Road; Monmouth; 503.838.6013

Hours: Sat–Sun 12:00pm-5:00pm (Mar-Dec)

Tasting Fee: FREE for 7 tastes

Wine: 7 varieties; $10.00–$30.00
Specializing in a range of unique wines

Outside: Surrounded by both vines and woods, with a small lake planted right in the middle, this is a perfect spot to have a picnic lunch. Bring something to grill on their barbeque and enjoy the shaded pavillion.

Inside: Smallish space with an inlaid wood wine bar that features the winery's logo—a hot air balloon. Have your tasting outside on the patio if possible.

Notes: The winery was named in honor of the hot air balloon tradition from France: When a hot air balloon lands in someone's field, a bottle of wine was given for the inconvenience! • Happiness simply radiates from the owner, Mary. Catch it if you can!

Facts: Established 1986 • 32 acres (planted) and other grapes are sourced from the area • Willamette Valley AVA • 8,000 cases annually

Owner: Mary Olson
Winemaker: Elizabeth Clark

Date visited: _____
Went with: _____
Notes: _____
_____

Ankeny Vineyard

view

fanciness

deck/patio

food for sale

picnic area

bus/rv

pet friendly

tours

event space

www.ankenyvineyard.com
2565 Riverside Drive South; Salem; 503.378.1498

Hours: Daily 11:00am–5:00pm (year-round)

Tasting Fee: $5.00 flight of 6-7 tastes

Wine: 7 varieties; $12.00-$20.00
Specializes in Pinot Noir and Maréchal Foch

Outside: Take the pretty, winding, quiet drive out to Ankeny and hang out for a while on their big outdoor deck – then take a hike! The owner, Joe, gives tours.

Inside: Friendly service by the Wine Duchess in this gussied up barn with true country character. There's a super-long tasting bar with windows giving you a full-time view. Fireplace seating in the winter.

Notes: Ask about the hiking path that leads you to a stellar picnic spot, gorgeous views, a pleasant pond, 1840's cemetery, llamas, and even emu too! • If you are a birdwatcher or nature fan, include a visit to nearby Ankeny Natural Wildlife Refuge. • Ankeny Vineyard was named for their position on Ankeny Hill.

Facts: Established 1982 • 35 acres • Willamette Valley AVA • 2,000 cases annually

Owner: Joe Olexa
Winemaker: Andy Thomas

Date visited: _____
Went with: _____
Notes: _____
_____

Cardwell Hill

● ●

www.cardwellhillwine.com
24241 Cardwell Hill Drive; Philomath; 541-929-WINE

Hours: Daily 12:00pm-5:30pm (May–Thanks)

Tasting Fee: $1.00 per taste, 4 wines featured

Wine: 4 varieties; $12.00–$32.00
Specializing in Pinot Noir

Outside: The white stone tasting room stands out amongst the beautiful natural surroundings. Bring a picnic lunch to sit, relax and take in the rolling hills that surround you from the outside terrace.

Inside: This newly redesigned tasting room takes European touches and melds them with Northwest style. Sip at the 14-foot-long oak bar surrounded by tables and chairs allowing everyone to enjoy viewing the vineyard while tasting wines.

Notes: The winery rests at the base of Cardwell Hill, hence the winery name. • The vineyard is certified sustainable LIVE and Salmon-Safe.

Facts: Established 2000 • 40 Acres • Willamette Valley AVA • 5,500 cases annually

Owners: Nancy and Dan Chapel
Winemaker: Dan Chapel

Date visited: _____
Went with: _____
Notes: _____
_____

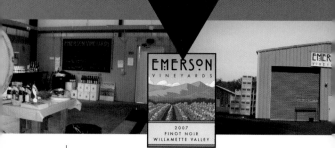

Emerson

view

fanciness

deck/patio

food for sale

picnic area

bus/rv

pet friendly

tours

event space

● ●

www.emersonvineyards.com
11665 Airlie Road; Monmouth; 503.838.0944

Hours: Sat-Sun 12:00pm-5:00pm (Mar-Dec)

Tasting Fee: $5.00 flight of 5 tastes

Wine: 5 varieties; $15.00–$25.00
Specializes in food friendly wines

Outside: Lots of beautiful trees, vines, and lush rolling hills give you a pleasant countryside view, until you step inside the winery/barn, which needs more (and bigger) windows and some kind of decoration.

Inside: Enjoy your tasting from within a working winery. The small, inlaid marble wine bar is situated right next to the wine vats, barrels, boxes and bottles.

Notes: This father and son duo started their winery – the son is the "wines and vines" side of the winery and dad runs the business and marketing side.
• Cheese and cracker nibbles are typically offered.
• Winery named in honor of the family's grandfather, Emerson Waldo Fisher. • Nice and colorful labels!

Facts: Established 2005 • 127 acres (25 producing) • Willamette Valley AVA • 3,500 cases annually

Owner: Tom Johns
Winemaker: Elliott Johns

Date visited: _____
Went with: _____
Notes: _____

Harris Bridge

www.harrisbridgevineyard.com
22937 Harris Road; Philomath; 541.929.3053

Hours: Sat–Sun 12:00pm-5:00pm (Jun-Oct)

Tasting Fee: $5.00–$10.00 flights of 3-7 tastes

Wine: 10 varieties; $23.00–$60.00
Specializes in dessert wines

Outside: You'll follow a long, gravel road to get here, but if you turned at the covered bridge sign, you *will* eventually arrive. The old, white, covered bridge gives personality and nostalgia to the place. Giant close-up hills give you even more of a view from porch or lawn.

Inside: It's contemporary and bright, yet still has an old-time, small-town barn-dance feel.

Notes: They have several older, library wines and a brandy distillery is on the way soon. • Bocce ball!
• Secret notes are wrapped around bottle tops.
• It's all dessert wines, so makes a perfect last stop.

Facts: Established 2001 • 4 acres (plus source grapes and fruit) • Willamette Valley AVA • 200-400 cases annually

Owners: Nathan Warren and Amada Sever
Winemakers: Nathan Warren and Amada Sever

Date visited: _____
Went with: _____
Notes: _____
_____

decor

food for sale

event space

gift shop

Honeywood Winery

www.honeywoodwinery.com
1350 Hines Street SE; Salem; 800.726.4101

Hours: Weekdays 9:00am–5:00pm;
Sat 10:00am–5:00pm; Sun 1:00pm–5:00pm (year-round)
(plus extended holiday hours for Christmas shopping)

Tasting Fee: FREE flight of 5 tastes

Wine: 50 varieties; $12.00-$24.00
Specializes in Fruit Wines and lots of them!

Notes: "Honeywood" comes from mixing the two
owners' names (Honeyman and Wood) and is even
more appropriate with their sweet wine series. It's
definitely reminiscent of going to an old-time candy
store! • There's an American grape series (aka Ben
Franklin wines) and Oregon area specialties too, like
cranberry or marionberry wines. Or try trendy healthy
fruit styles like blueberry or pomegranate. • There is
a huge gift shop here with all kinds of wine-related
paraphernalia and food baskets for gifts or picnics.

Facts: Established 1934 • 20 acres in West Salem
(plus sources grapes and fruit from all over OR & WA)
• Willamette Valley AVA • 30,000 cases annually

Owners: John Wood and Ron Honeyman
Winemakers: Marlene and Paul Gallick

Date visited: _____
Went with: _____
Notes: _____

view

ciness

Marks Ridge

••••••••••••••••••••••••••••

www.marksridge.com
29255 Berlin Road; Sweet Home; 541.367.3292

k/patio

Hours: Wed–Sun 12:00pm-6:00pm (summer);
Call for hours off-season

Tasting Fee: $3.00 flight of 5 tastes

for sale

Wine: 4 varieties; $16.00–$28.00
Specializes in German styles and Pinot Noir

nic area

Outside: Head for the hills then head to the porch!
Take Pleasant Valley off Hwy. 20, veer right to Berlin.

us/rv

Inside: A long wall of windows allows you to see all of
the outside from the inside (but you'll want to be out).

Notes: Named for its position way up high on Marks
Ridge. • Standing alone on its own out east. Keep it
in mind for a visit sometime when heading to or from
Bend. Or maybe just make a day of it sometime!

friendly

• Check website calendar for Music and Art events.
• There's food for sale and it's a great place for lunch.

Facts: Established 2007 • 57 acres (12 producing
with 1970's plantings) • Willamette Valley AVA
• 1,000 cases annually

nt space

Owners: Jay and Janet Westly
Winemaker: Jay Westly

Date visited: _____
Went with: _____
Notes: _____
_____

view

fanciness

deck/patio

food for sale

picnic area

bus/rv

pet friendly

tours

event space

Piluso

• •

www.pilusowines.com
6654 Shaw Hwy SE; Aumsville; 503.749.4125

Hours: Sat–Sun 12:00pm-6:00pm (May–Oct)

Tasting Fee: FREE flight of 4 tastes

Wine: 4-6 varieties; $20.00–$30.00
Specializes in Gamay Noir Blanc and Pinot Noir

Outside: Fantastic secret wine garden with a little "magic cottage" to enjoy inside or out. It *is* a farm, but pretty much everything here is super-cute!

Inside: Discover your favorite pick for a picnic at the small, welcoming tasting room at the far end from the quaint, yellow farmhouse.

Notes: The wine is named after the family name, particularly after Pinky's grandparents, who are rumored to have made wine in the early 1900s for Portland's Italian community. • The rest of the story of Piluso's creation is the opposite of "Green Acres," with wife Sandy being the country girl dragging her city-boy hubby out to the country. Now he loves it!

Facts: Established 2000 • 65 acres (4 producing) • Willamette Valley AVA • 500 cases annually

Owners: Sandee and Pinky Piluso
Winemaker: Sandee Piluso

Date visited: _____
Went with: _____
Notes: _____
_____

Spindrift

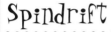

• •

www.spindriftcellars.com
810 Applegate Street; Philomath; 541.929.6555

Hours: Tue-Fri 1:00pm-6:00pm; Sat-Sun 12:00pm-5:00pm (wine season); Fri 12:00pm-6:00pm; Sat-Sun 12:00pm-5:00pm (winter)

Tasting Fee: $4.00 for 4 tastes (red or white) or $6.00 for all

Wine: 14 varieties; $13.00–$38.00
Specializing in Pinot Noir and Pinot Gris

Notes: Easy access just off Hwy. 34 on the way to the coast, and "Spindrift" is appropriately named for such an occassion. After much discussion, it was owner Tabitha's grandfather, who said the wine was a step above, like the mist on top of the wave, the "spindrift."• Inside the tasting room (located next-door to the winery itself), the focal point is a beautiful hand-painted mural of the Spindrift logo. • The tasting bar rests on very cool black-and-copper painted wine barrels—shabby chic! • The vineyards are LIVE and Salmon-Safe certified.

Facts: Established 2005 • 30 acres • Willamette Valley AVA • 3,500 cases annually

Owners: Matt and Tabitha Compton
Winemaker: Matt Compton

Date visited: _____
Went with: _____
Notes: _____
_____

view

fanciness

deck/patio

food for sale

picnic area

bus/rv

pet friendly

tours

event space

Springhill Cellars

· ·

www.springhillcellars.com
2920 NW Scenic View Drive; Albany; 541.928.1009

Hours: Sat–Sun 1:00pm-5:00pm (May–Nov)

Tasting Fee: FREE flight of 2-5 tastes

Wine: 2-5 varieties; $15.00-$20.00
Specializes in Pinot Noir and Pinot Gris

Outside: Plan for a picnic here with triple-tier views of the vineyard, then the McDonald Forest, then the Coastal Range. Marvelous views!

Inside: Very simple tasting room lined with barrels.

Notes: Named after its location on the slope of Springhill, a small hill on the banks of the Willamette River. Was it destined at birth? Co-owner's name means sea + wine in French (Mer-vin). • Various paper collages on wine labels created by artist and neighbor Anna Tewes.

Facts: Established 1988 (some 1978 plantings) • 20 acres from two vineyards in the Willamette Valley AVA • 1,000–1,200 cases annually

Owners: Mike and Karen McLain with Karen's father, Merv Anthony
Winemaker: Mike McLain

Date visited: _____
Went with: _____
Notes: _____
_____

iew

ciness

/patio

for sale

ic area

us/rv

friendly

ours

t space

Silver Falls Vineyards

• •

www.silverfallsvineyards.com
4972 Cascade Hwy SE; Sublimity; 503.769.5056

Hours: Fri-Sun 11:00am-6:00pm (May–Sep);
Sat-Sun 11:00am-6:00pm (Oct-Apr, closed Jan)

Tasting Fee: $5.00 flight of 6+ tastes

Wine: 10 varieties; $10.00–$16.00
Specializing in well-priced everyday wines

Outside: You'll pass sheep, chickens and even llamas
out here in the country. It's all very open and green,
and all quite flat. Nice gazebo and tables out back.

Inside: Small tasting room and bar, but with a big
party room and small gift shop with good stuff.

Notes: Named for the nearby Silver Falls State Park,
where you can take a nice hike and see more than
10 waterfalls! Or, check out Oregon Gardens and the
nearby antique town of Sublimity. • They love doing
weddings and parties here.

Facts: Established 2000 • 20 acres (1970s plantings)
• Willamette Valley AVA • 2,000 cases annually

Owner: Duane Defrees
Winemaker: Andreas Wetzel

Date visited: _____
Went with: _____
Notes: _____
_____

view

fanciness

deck/patio

food for sale

picnic area

bus/rv

pet friendly

tours

event space

Tyee

•••••••••••••••••••••••••••

www.tyeewine.com
26335 Greenberry Road; Corvallis; 541.753.8754

Hours: Fri-Mon 12:00pm-5:00pm (Jun–Sep);
Sat-Sun 12:00pm-5:00pm (Oct-Jun)

Tasting Fee: FREE flight 5 tastes

Wine: 5 varieties; $15.00–$25.00
Specializing in well-balanced food wines

Outside: I love the feel of this place inside and out.
Behind the barn is a large outdoor concert area and
outdoor bar, so be sure to check their online calendar.

Inside: In its previous life, this space was the original
milking parlor for a dairy farm. Now it is home to both
wine and a small art gallery.

Notes: The Buchanan family has lived on the farm,
now winery, for five generations—and counting.
• The name "Tyee" comes from the NW Indian word
meaning: chief, biggest, best! • Their labels display
cool Northwest-style art by James Jordan. • Organic
and Salmon-Safe • Check their website for parties.

Facts: Established 1985 • 10 acres • Willamette
Valley AVA • 1,500 cases annually

Owners: Dave and Margy Buchanan
Winemaker: Merrilee Buchanan

Date visited: _____
Went with: _____
Notes: _____
_____

Viridian

Olsen Family Vineyards

www.viridianwines.com
8930 Suver Road; Monmouth; 503.838.2022

Hours: Sat–Sun 12:00pm-5:00pm (Jun-Nov)

Tasting Fee: FREE flight of 5 tastes

Wine: 5 varieties; $12.00–$18.00
Specializes in Pinot Noir

Outside: Expansive land in the flats right off the highway.
Tastings outside is the only way to go here.

Inside: The inside IS the outside! Everything is set up
inside a summer Tasting Pavilion tent. Tastings also by
appointment other times of the year.

Notes: Olsen family pride shines through five generations of agriculture going back to the early 1800's.
• The wines are made with 100% estate grapes.
Also on their property are blueberries, peppermint,
philbert orchards and a nursery.

Facts: Established 2006 • 510 acres (180 producing)
• Willamette Valley AVA • 15,000 cases annually

Owners: The Olsen Family
Winemaker: Bill Kremer

Date visited: _____
Went with: _____
Notes: _____
_____

view

fanciness

deck/patio

food for sale

picnic area

bus/rv

pet friendly

tours

event space

Willamette Valley

www.willamettevalleyvineyards.com
8800 Enchanted Way SE; Turner; 800.344.9463

Hours: Daily 11:00am–6:00pm (year-round)

Tasting Fee: FREE flight of 5 tastes; $6.00 Reserve flight of 6 tastes (keep the Riedel glass)

Wine: 15–20 varieties; $10.00–$50.00 Specializes in Pinot Noir

Outside: Truly a majestic and commanding presence up high on the hill, with gorgeous views overlooking the valley below. Lots of picnic space and great deck!

Inside: Super-long party bar in nice, yet friendly space.

Notes: Easy access right off Hwy. 5 makes it hard *not* to stop, once you know how special this place is
• Scheduled tours at 11:00am, 2:00pm and 4:00pm ($15.00 each; must RSVP at least 48 hrs. ahead).
• Their wine bottles made special appearances many times on the set of "Friends". • Eco-Conscious, LIVE and Salmon-Safe certified; glass and cork recycling.

Facts: Established 1983 • 53 on-site acres (producing)
• Willamette Valley AVA • 120,000 cases (including their other wines, Tualatin Estates and Griffin Creek)

Owner: Jim Bernau
Winemakers: Forrest Klaffke and Don Crank III

Date visited: _____
Went with: _____
Notes: _____

Eugene/Lane County Map

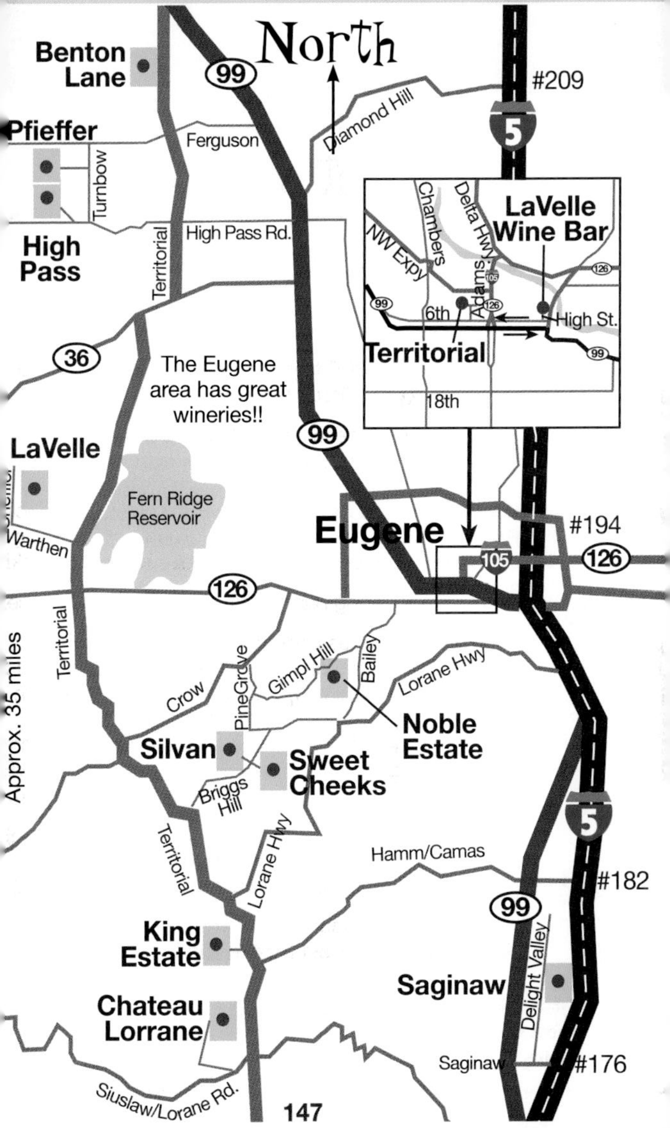

North
Benton Lane
Pfieffer
High Pass
Turnbow
Ferguson
Diamond Hill
#209
5
High Pass Rd.
Territorial
99
36
The Eugene area has great wineries!!
LaVelle Wine Bar
Chambers
Delta Hwy
NW Expy
Adams
105
126
6th
High St.
Territorial
18th
LaVelle
Fern Ridge Reservoir
Warthen
Eugene
#194
126
Crow
PineGrove
Gimpl Hill
Bailey
Lorane Hwy
Noble Estate
Silvan
Sweet Cheeks
Briggs Hill
Approx. 35 miles
Hamm/Camas
#182
Lorane Hwy
King Estate
Chateau Lorrane
Saginaw
Delight Valley
Saginaw
#176
Siuslaw/Lorane Rd.

view

fanciness

deck/patio

food for sale

picnic area

bus/rv

pet friendly

tours

event space

Benton-Lane Winery

www.benton-lane.com
23924 Territorial Hwy.; Monroe; 541.847.5792

Hours: Mon–Fri 11:00am–4:30pm (year-round);
plus Sat–Sun 11:00am–5:00pm (Apr–Nov)

Tasting Fee: FREE flight 2-4 tastes

Wine: 2-4 varieties; $16.00–$26.00
Specializing in Pinot Gris and Pinot Noir

Outside: The original land was called "Sunnymount Ranch," which seems exactly right when you approach this barn-like winery complex positioned high up on a most-likely sun-filled hill. Nice back picnic patio!

Inside: That upscale-rustic,-Northwest-barn look with high, beamed ceilings and double French doors.

Notes: Due to its position directly east of the highest peaks in the Cascade mountains, it lies in the "rain shadow" and gets sunnier slopes. • The label name comes from its location between both Benton and Lane counties. • LIVE and Salmon-Safe certified. • See website for their recent awards and press!

Facts: Established 1992 • 318 acres total (148 acres planted) • Willamette Valley AVA • 25,000 cases

Owners: Steve and Carol Girard
Winemaker: Christopher Mazepink

Date visited: _____
Went with: _____
Notes: _____
_____

148

Chateau Lorane

• •

www.chateaulorane.com
27415 Siuslaw River Road; Lorane; 541.942.8028

Hours: Daily 12:00pm–5:00pm (summer);
Sat–Sun 12:00pm–5:00pm (off-season)

Tasting Fee: FREE flight 6+ tastes

Wine: 30 varieties; $12.00–$25.00
Specializing in variety including Baco Noir and Meads

Outside: Overlooks Lake Louise from way up high!
Nice big wooden deck where you can be shaded just
enough by towering fir trees or the roof overhead.

Inside: Pretty basic, big interior with two very long,
wooden tasting bars and glass award showcases.

Notes: Many, *many* wines with some exciting surprises
(they like to blend and have fun). Lots of fruit wines
too. • Secluded special events facility for all kinds
of party needs! • A peaceful country, friendly escape.
• Named after the nearby township of Lorane.

Facts: Established 1991 • Sits on 220 acres, but sources
grapes from throughout the Willamette Valley AVA •
5,000 cases annually

Owners: Linde and Sharon Kester
Winemaker: David Hook

Date visited: _____
Went with: _____
Notes: _____

_____

view

fanciness

deck/patio

food for sale

picnic area

bus/rv

pet friendly

tours

event space

High Pass Winery

www.highpasswinery.com
24757 Lavell Road; Junction City; 541.998.1447

Hours: Fri–Sun 12:00pm–5:00pm (May–Nov) and by appt.

Tasting Fee: FREE flight 6+ tastes

Wine: 10 varieties; $10.00–$25.00
Specializing in unique German styles

Outside: Most definitely out there in the country, but only sorta kinda high.

Inside: Fresh, clean, white walls with high ceilings and skylights, simple style with natural wood trim and several pieces of art.

Notes: From website, they represent "a modern European viticulture approach, yielding high quality wines at attractive prices."

Facts: Established 1984 • 20 acres • Willamette Valley AVA • 1,000 cases

Owner: Dieter Boehm
Winemaker: Dieter Boehm

Date visited: _____
Went with: _____
Notes: _____
_____

view

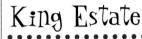

ciness

k/patio

for sale

King Estate
•••••••••••••••••••••••••••••

www.kingsestate.com
80854 Territorial Road; Eugene; 800.884.4441

Hours: Daily 11:00am-8:00pm (until 9:00pm all summer) Late-night award winners!

Tasting Fee: $5.00 Flight of 4 tastes

Wine: 7 varieties; $12.00-$35.00
Specializes in Pinot Noir and Pinot Gris

nic area

us/rv

friendly

tours

Outside: Extremely impressive hilltop estate! It's all very obviously fit for a king from the long, curvy, paved road, to the immaculate, grand architecture, to the giant terraces with commanding views. It's a stand-out showpiece (expect a crowd).

Inside: Huge and stately tasting room with peeks at two fine dining rooms with fireplaces and views.

Notes: All organically farmed with on-site orchards, olive trees and vegetable gardens for the restaurant.
• Originally founded by the King family. • Premier conference, wedding and party facilities!

Facts: Established 1991 • 1,000+ acres (465 acres vines) • Willamette Valley AVA • 175,000 cases

nt space

Owner: Ed Keye
Winemakers: John Elhow / Lindsay Boudreaux / Jeff Kandarian

Date visited: _____
Went with: _____
Notes: _____

view

fanciness

deck/patio

food for sale

picnic area

bus/rv

pet friendly

tours

event space

La Velle

• •

www.lavellevineyards.com
89697 Sheffler Road; Elmira; 541.935.9406

Hours: Daily 12:00pm-5:00pm (year-round)

Tasting Fee: FREE Flight of 6+ tastes

Wine: 15 varieties; $16.00-$30.00
Specializes in Riesling and Pinot Noir

Outside: Private and secluded, landscaped, terraced
gardens with tables set-up in a small grotto. There's
lots of grass for picnicking and relaxing in lawn chairs.

Inside: New, Northwest-chalet style with an extra-long
tasting bar in an open room with several big windows.

Notes: They like to be involved with local community
music and art groups and do some fun events like a
Murder Mystery Theater – check their website.

Facts: Established 1984 • 8 acres (plus sourced local
and Columbia Valley grapes) • Willamette Valley AVA
• 40,000 cases

Owner: Doug LaVelle
Winemaker: Matthew LaVelle

LaVelle Wine Bar
296 E. 5th Street (Downtown Eugene)
541.338-9875 Sat–Tues 12-6pm and Wed–Fri 3-9pm

Date visited: _____
Went with: _____
Notes: _____
_____

view

ciness

k/patio

for sale

nic area

us/rv

friendly

tours

nt space

Noble Estate

• •

www.nobleestatevineyard.com
29210 Gimpl Hill Road; Eugene; 541.954.9870

Hours: Sat–Sun 12:00pm-5:00pm (year-round)

Tasting Fee: $5.00 Flight of 6+ tastes

Wine: 14–16 varieties; $12.00-$30.00
Specializes in variety

Outside: What a delightful surprise to get to enjoy a tropical paradise in the middle of Oregon! There's a wooden viewing deck with lots of tables, and an elevated gazebo with a comfy party platform *and* a brilliant turquoise pool, all surrounded by palm trees, distant vistas and gorgeous gardens. No swimming.

Inside: Tastefully decorated like a nice wine bar with red walls, thick Oriental rugs and comfy couches. Windows are everywhere to bring the outside in.

Notes: Believe in meticulous nurturing of the grapes as they grow. • Pool for show only.

Facts: Established 1999 • 3 acres (plus sourced local and Rogue Valley grapes) • Willamette Valley AVA • 2,700 cases

Owners: Mark and Marie Jurasevich
Winemaker: Mark Jurasevich

Date visited: _____
Went with: _____
Notes: _____
_____

view

fanciness

deck/patio

food for sale

picnic area

bus/rv

pet friendly

tours

event space

Pfeiffer
• •

www.pfeiffervineyards.com
25040 Jaeg Road; Junction City; 541-998-2828

Hours: Wed–Sun 11:00am-5:00pm (year-round)

Tasting Fee: $10.00 Whites and $20.00 for Reserve Pinot Noirs (includes Pinot clinic inside Private Grotto). Keep your commemorative Riedel wine goblet.

Wine: 13 varieties; $16.00-$60.00
Specializes in Pinot Noir

Outside: Basic barn exterior does not reflect inside.

Inside: Fabulous caves and Tuscan *style!* There is just so much here and the surprise factor will be fun!

Notes: Be sure to go to their website and find info on indulgent "Villa Evenings," Cave Party "Rites of Passage" and of course, weddings. • In the 70's, "the French called" and changed everything! More recently, their wine was served as part of inaugural celebrations – and that just might change everything too. • Totally solar-powered. • Delicious chocolates and cheeses served. • A very special place!

Facts: Established 2001 (1983 plantings) • 70 acres (producing) • Willamette Valley AVA • 1,200 cases

Owners: Robin and Danuta Pfeiffer
Winemaker: Robin Pfeiffer

Date visited: _____
Went with: _____
Notes: _____
_____

Saginaw Vineyard

• •

www.saginawvineyard.com
80247 Delight Valley; Cottage Grove; 541.942.1364

Hours: Daily 11:00am-5:00pm (year-round);
Friday night summer 6:00pm-9:00pm concert series

Tasting Fee: FREE for 7 tastes

Wine: 7 varieties; $12.00-$27.00
Specializes in farm-fresh fruit wines

Outside: Back-to-basics farm charm here with an old turn-of-the-century home and attached barn. Lots of lawn and wide-open spaces.

Inside: Tasting room could be right out of the Mayberry RFD TV show, housed in an old 1906 barn. There's a gift shop with Oregon jellies & syrups, hazelnuts, and candy. Ask about making your own wine labels!

Notes: Check their website for Friday night concert schedule going all summer. • One acre of blueberries planted on-site. • Named for surrounding Saginaw area.

Facts: Established 2001 • 35 acres (9 producing from 1992 plantings) • Willamette Valley AVA • 1,500-2,000 cases

Owners: Scott and Cheryl Byler
Winemakers: Scott Byler and Sheryl Zettle

Date visited: _____
Went with: _____
Notes: _____
_____

Sidebar icons:
ew
iness
/patio
for sale
c area
s/rv
riendly
ours
t space

view

fanciness

deck/patio

food for sale

picnic area

bus/rv

pet friendly

tours

event space

Silvan Ridge / Hinman
• •

www.silvanridge.com
27012 Briggs Hill Road; Eugene; 541.345.1945

Hours: Daily 12:00pm-5:00pm (year-round)

Tasting Fee: FREE for up to 7 tastes ($2.00 extras)

Wine: 13 varieties; $15.00-$40.00
Specializes in Pinot Noir and Early Muscat

Outside: Gorgeous exterior and the outside is where you want to be! Enjoy veranda viewing at its finest.

Inside: Soaring wood-beamed ceilings, giant arches, and walls of windows to catch the views outside. Plus party rooms you can sneak off to and enjoy big group tables, couches or even a fireplace.

Notes: Named after Silva, the maiden name of owner, plus Silvan means wooded. • There are two brands here, the Hinman label produced deliciously at a lower price point.• Indoor and outdoor exclusive rental facilities.

Facts: Established 1979 • 5 acres (sources from diverse areas in W. Oregon) • Willamette Valley AVA • 30,000 cases annually

Owners: Doyle Hinman (original owner); Currently owned by Elizabeth Chambers
Winemaker: Jonathan Oberlander

Date visited: _____
Went with: _____
Notes: _____

Sweet Cheeks

• •

view

nciness

ck/patio

d for sale

nic area

ous/rv

t friendly

tours

nt space

www.sweetcheekswinery.com
27007 Briggs Hill Road; Eugene; 541.349.9463

Hours: Daily 12:00pm-6:00pm (year-round);
Twilight tastings on Fridays until 9:00pm

Tasting Fee: FREE for 4 tastes

Wine: 8 varieties; $12.00-$22.00
Specializes in Rieslings and Pinot Noir

Outside: Enjoy the sweet life and plant your cheeks at one of many tables outside on the stellar outdoor patio. From your elevated position way up high, see what shapes you can find in the clouds and hills!

Inside: Gorgeous, old-world space with big, fun bar.

Notes: Label gets its name from the shape the ravine forms while looking at it from across the valley (if you squint, use your imagination, and maybe drink a bit of wine, it *does* form "sweet cheeks"). • The crow on the label comes from its proximity to nearby Crow Valley. • You can buy a packaged lunch for two and enjoy a truly fantastic picnic here!

Facts: Established 2004 (1978 plantings) • 145 acres (65 in grapes) • Willamette Valley AVA • 10,000 cases

Owners: Dan Smith and Lorrie Normann
Winemaker: Mark Nicholl

Date visited: _____
Went with: _____
Notes: _____
_____

decor

food for sale

event space

gift shop

Territorial

• •

www.territorialvineyards.com
907 West Third Avenue; Eugene; 541.684.9463

Hours: Fri-Sat 5:00pm–9:00pm
Thur 5:00pm–11:00pm (with live music)

Tasting Fee: $7.00 for 7 tastes

Wine: 4 varieties; $15.00-$30.00
Specializes in estate-grown varietals

Notes: Former coffee warehouse turned café-cool,
hot, urban winery. Located a couple blocks east of
the Blair Boulevard Historic District in the fun and
funky Whiteaker neighborhood. • Officially known
as Territorial Vineyards & Wine Company, named
after the Lane County territorial corridor where their
vineyards reside. • The labels pick up on map-style
graphics. • Try and catch the live music on Thursday
nights or the last Friday art walk. Fun place!

Facts: Established 2001 • 28 acres (off-site estate
vineyards) • Willamette Valley AVA • 1,200 cases

Owners: Jeff Willson and Victoria Charles-Wilson;
Alan and April Mitchell
Winemaker: John Jarboe

Date visited: _____
Went with: _____
Notes: _____
_____

Umpqua/North Map

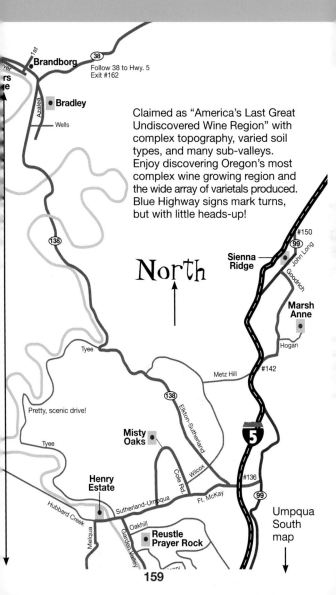

Brandborg

(38) Follow 38 to Hwy. 5 Exit #162

Bradley

Wells

Claimed as "America's Last Great Undiscovered Wine Region" with complex topography, varied soil types, and many sub-valleys. Enjoy discovering Oregon's most complex wine growing region and the wide array of varietals produced. Blue Highway signs mark turns, but with little heads-up!

North

↑

(138)

#150

(99) Sienna Ridge

John Long

Goodrich

Marsh Anne

Hogan

Tyee

Metz Hill #142

Pretty, scenic drive!

(138)

Elkton-Sutherland

Tyee

Misty Oaks

Cole Rd.

Wilcox

5

#136

Henry Estate

Sutherland-Umpqua

Ft. McKay

(99)

Hubbard Creek

Melqua

Oakhill

Garden Valley

Reustle Prayer Rock

Umpqua South map

↓

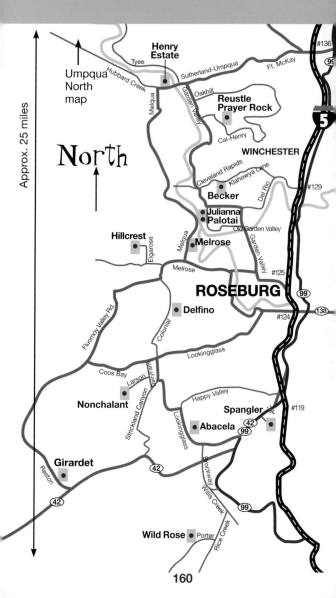

Approx. 25 miles

Umpqua North map

North

Henry Estate

Tyee

Hubbard Creek

Sutherland-Umpqua

Ft. McKay

#136

99

Oakhill

Reustle Prayer Rock

Garden Valley

Melqua

Cal-Henry

WINCHESTER

5

Cleveland Rapids

Klahowya Lane

Del Rio

#129

Becker

Julianna Palotai

Old Garden Valley

Hillcrest

Elgarose

Melqua

Melrose

Melrose

Garden Valley

#125

ROSEBURG

99

138

Delfino

#124

Colonial

Fluornoy Valley Rd.

Lookingglass

Coos Bay

Larson

Nonchalant

Strickland Canyon

Berry Farm

Happy Valley

Lookingglass

Spangler

#119

Abacela

42

99

42

Girardet

Reston

42

Brockway

Willis Creek

99

Wild Rose Porter

Rice Creek

160

iew

ciness

k/patio

for sale

ic area

us/rv

friendly

ours

t space

Abacela

• •

www.abacela.com
12500 Lookingglass Road; Roseburg; 541.679.6642

Hours: Daily 11:00am-5:00pm (year-round)

Tasting Fee: $5.00 for 5 tastes

Wine: 16 varieties; $14.00–$30.00
Specializes in Spanish varietals

Outside: Spectacular vistas with fresh breezes from high on the hill. Plan on lunch in one of two romantic gazebos! Tasting room building adds a bit of Spanish-style atmosphere with stucco and terra cotta.

Inside: Small and cozy Spanish-style wine bar with tan stucco walls, natural woods and a huge "Abacela" barrel sign. It's a big shame you have to miss their incredible view without big front windows there!

Notes: Name comes from the Spanish word *abacelar*, which means to plant a grapevine. • 100% estate wines. • They were the first American winery to win an International Tempranillo competition. • They share the same latitude positioning as northern Spain.

Facts: Established 1997 • 500 acres (60 producing) • Umpqua Valley AVA • 10,000 cases annually

Owners: Earl and Hilda Jones
Winemaker: Andrew Wenzl

Date visited: _____
Went with: _____
Notes: _____

view

fanciness

deck/patio

food for sale

picnic area

bus/rv

pet friendly

tours

event space

Becker

•••••••••••••••••••••••••••

www.beckerwine.com
360 Klahowya Lane; Roseburg; 541.677.0288

Hours: Daily 11:00am–5:00pm (year-round)

Tasting Fee: FREE for 4 tastes

Wine: 7-9 varieties; $17.00–$30.00
Specializes in Müller-Thurgau and Pinot Noir Rosé

Outside: This white, barn-style tasting room with a bright red roof sits peacefully surrounded by tree-covered hills on all sides. Wine-drinking visitors quickly liven up the place by playing with the dogs and enjoying the sun on the outdoor wooden deck.

Inside: Light and bright, newly constructed and freshly painted room with soaring A-frame ceilings covered with wood. Open French doors lead out to the porch.

Notes: The Beckers personally worked *really* hard and planted all their own vines. • 100% estate wines. • Dry farming (no man-made irrigation). • Horseshoe and bocce pits coming soon.

Facts: Established 2008 • 10 acres (planted in year 2000) • Umpqua Valley AVA • 700 cases annually

Owners: Charlie and Peggy Becker (and of course, with their dog, Müller)
Winemaker: Charlie Becker

Date visited: _____
Went with: _____
Notes: _____
_____

view

nciness

ck/patio

d for sale

nic area

ous/rv

t friendly

tours

ent space

Bradley Vineyards

. . . .

www.bradleyvineyards.com
1000 Azalea Drive; Elkton; 541.584.2888

Hours: Wed–Sun 11:00am-5:00pm (Jun–Nov)

Tasting Fee: FREE for 6 tastes

Wine: 7 varieties; $14.00–$28.00
Specializes in estate grown grapes

Outside: Very sweet farm with cute little blue house.
Follow the "Route-66-Burma-Shave"-style signs up
the hill to the tasting room. There's a raised, wooden
deck for marveling at the view while sitting, sipping
and sunning!

Inside: Back to basics. Small, simple room with
single table-top tastings.

Notes: Occasional summer events and they do
weddings too. • Sells 95% of their grapes to other
vineyards. • Don't miss the Baco Noir!

Facts: Established 2001 (1983 plantings) • 25 acres
• Umpqua Valley AVA • 500 cases annually

Owners: John and Bonnie Bradley
Winemaker: John Bradley

Date visited: _____
Went with: _____
Notes: _____
_____

view

fanciness

deck/patio

food for sale

picnic area

bus/rv

pet friendly

tours

event space

Brandborg

• •

www.brandborgwine.com
345 First Street; Elkton; 541.584.2870

Hours: Daily 11:00am-5:00pm (Mem–Thanks);
plus by appointment other times

Tasting Fee: $5.00 for 6+ tastes

Wine: 12 varieties; $14.00–$30.00
Specializes in Pinot Noir and cool climate varietals

Outside: Right off Hwy. 38 and if it's not already, it
will soon become a "required" stop along the way to
or from the coast! Right on the main street in town,
there's a nice patio to enjoy outside.

Inside: Spacious, light, gallery-like room with quality,
local artwork and other prints. Music stage for occasional
concerts and second story seating available too. Gifts.

Notes: Deli snack items available seasonally. • Ask
about recent press and awards! • Also ask about the
"Love Puppets," based on the owners' own fairytale
love story. Cute.

Facts: Established 2002 • 60 acres (5 producing)
Umpqua Valley AVA • Also sources from other local
vineyards • 7,500 cases annually

Owners: Terry and Sue Brandborg
Winemakers: Terry and Sue Brandborg

Date visited: _____

Went with: _____

Notes: _____

_____

iew

ciness

x/patio

for sale

ic area

us/rv

riendly

ours

t space

Chateau Nonchalant

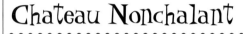

www.chateaunonchalantvineyards.com
1329 Larson Road; Roseburg; 541.679.2394

Hours: Fri–Sun 11:00am-5:00pm (Apr–Nov);
plus by appointment other times

Tasting Fee: FREE for 4 tastes

Wine: 4 varieties; $19.00–$25.00
Specializes in Pinot Noir

Outside: Peaceful and country-quiet (although, rumor
is, the vineyard sings)! Relax on the outdoor, covered
patio with views of mountains, vineyards and horses.
Swimmable pond anticipated for late-summer 2009.

Inside: You are immediately transported to Italy with
the gorgeous old-world decor of the tasting room!

Notes: Named after owner's reputable, non-chalant
attitude and philosophies. • That baby angel on the
label is Bacchus, the Greek/Roman god of wine and
revelry (aka Dionysus). • On-site horse stable with
rescue horses (ask about both angel and horse stories).

Facts: Established 2003 • 50 acres (8 producing)
• Umpqua Valley AVA • 2,000 cases annually

Owners: Vicki and Weldon Manning; Randy Kohler
Winemaker: Scott Henry VI

Date visited: _____
Went with: _____
Notes: _____
_____

view

fanciness

deck/patio

food for sale

picnic area

bus/rv

pet friendly

tours

event space

Delfino

• •

www.delfinovineyards.com
3829 Colonial Road; Roseburg; 541.673.7575

Hours: Fri–Sun 11:00am-5:00pm (Mem-Thanks);
plus by appointment other times

Tasting Fee: FREE for 4 tastes

Wine: 4 varieties; $15.00–$26.00
Specializes in award-winning Syrah

Outside: You'll drive past a nice little lake and will
plan on buying a bottle even before you've tasted.
"Taste the place" is their tagline for a reason!

Inside: Brand spankin' new tasting room opened
mid-June 2009. Refined simplicity with neutral colors.

Notes: Their website says it all: "Come enjoy our
charming guest cottage, beautiful views and warm
country hospitality." Truly! For a memorable retreat,
treat yourself to a stay in the Delfino B&B (complete
with a bottle of wine and hot tub). • Delfino means
"dolphin" in Italian, thus the art adorning their label.

Facts: Established 2006 • 18 acres • Umpqua Valley
AVA • < 500 cases annually

Owners: Terri and Jim Delfino
Winemaker: Scott Henry VI

Date visited: _____
Went with: _____
Notes: _____
_____

view

nciness

ck/patio

d for sale

nic area

us/rv

friendly

tours

nt space

Girardet

• •

www.girardetwine.com
895 Reston Road; Roseburg; 541.679.7252

Hours: Daily 11:00am–5:00pm (year-round)

Tasting Fee: FREE for 6+ tastes

Wine: 11 varieties; $14.00–$25.00
Specializes in Baco Noir

Outside: Nice, big, expansive views of the entire area with a Swiss wood-cedar cabin tasting room. Picnic area with BBQ overlooking the vineyards.

Inside: Very simple and friendly tasting room with while walls, natural woods, and seating at the L-shaped bar or café tables and chairs.

Notes: The vineyard now totals 35 acres of over 30 varieties of grapes. • Dry farmed using sustainable methods and European craftsmanship. Hand harvests. • On the historic Coos Bay wagon road from 1872.

Facts: Established 1983 • 35 acres (some vines from 1971; occasionally sources grapes from neighbors) • Umpqua Valley AVA • 12,000 cases annually

Owners: Philippe and Bonnie Girardet
Winemaker: Marc Girardet

Date visited: _____
Went with: _____
Notes: _____
_____

view

fanciness

deck/patio

food for sale

picnic area

bus/rv

pet friendly

tours

event space

Henry Estate

• •

www.henryestate.com
687 Hubbard Creek Road; Umpqua; 541.459.5120

Hours: Daily 11:00am-5:00pm (year-round)

Tasting Fee: FREE for 5 tastes

Wine: 11 varieties; $10.00–$30.00
Specializes in Pinot Noir and Pinot Gris

Outside: If you like flowers, you'll love Henry Estate's gardens and landscaping. Sit back and relax on the trellissed porch with views of the expansive, sprawling lawn and distant hills.

Inside: A collection of "Greatest of the Grape" posters and other signs and prints blanket the walls, and dark brown paneling peeks out everywhere else.

Notes: Five generations of the Henry family have farmed the Umpqua Valley, and currently three generations run the estate. • Plan ahead to enjoy some extra memorial time in the memory garden, dedicated to the owner's grandparents.

Facts: Established 1980 • 40 acres • Umpqua Valley AVA • 8,000 cases annually

Owners: The Henry Family (Calvin Scott Henry III founder; inventor of the Scott Henry Trellis System)
Winemaker: Scott Henry IV

Date visited: _____

Went with: _____

Notes: _____

_____

ew

ciness

/patio

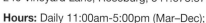
for sale

HillCrest

www.hillcrestvineyard.com
240 Vineyard Lane; Roseburg; 541.673.3709

Hours: Daily 11:00am-5:00pm (Mar–Dec);
plus by appointment Jan–Feb

Tasting Fee: FREE for 6+ tastes

Wine: 12 varieties; $24.00–$36.00
Specializes in classic style; old, dry-farmed vineyards

Outside: Big trees, old vines and a beautiful view of
the Callahan Mountain range! Big, green roof covers
the Swiss-chalet-style winery up on the crest of the hill.

Inside: Lodge-like interior with low ceilings and big,
wood beams. An older barn with lots of character.

Notes: From their website: "Good wines taste like
a grape. Great wines taste like a place." • Dyson's
theories, natural techniques and revolutionary, scien-
tific experiments lead to delicious success! • There
are no employees here (it's all family and friends).
• Site of Oregon's oldest estate winery and very first
Pinot Noir. A special place that's in good hands.

Facts: Established 2003 • 45 acres (13 producing;
1961 plantings) • Umpqua Valley AVA • 1,400 cases

Owners: Dyson and Susan DeMara
Winemaker: Dyson DeMara

Date visited: _____
Went with: _____
Notes: _____
_____

Julianna Vineyards

view

fanciness

deck/patio

food for sale

picnic area

bus/rv

pet friendly

tours

event space

www.juliannavineyards.com
707 Hess Lane; Roseburg, OR 97470; 541.677.9251

Hours: Sat–Sun 11:00am-5:00pm (Mem–Thanks); plus by appointment (off-season)

Tasting Fee: $2.00 for 4 tastes (if they remember)

Wine: 4 varieties; $12.00–$15.00
Specializes in good wines and a good price

Outside: Located right on the Umpqua River for outdoor tastings! This beautiful river also gives them a fertile microclimate for growing grapes.

Inside: There IS no inside! Well, in the summer anyway. When it's too cold outside, tastings are set up in a small tasting room in the winery building.

Notes: Locally produced cheese and fruit plates for sale in summer. • They make Bordeaux varietals and are a self-declared "Pinot-free zone." • 100% estate wines. • Ask about the Fizzé!

Facts: Established 2007 (1979 plantings) • 22 acres • Umpqua Valley AVA • 1,000 cases annually

Owners: Henry and Debbie Russel
Winemakers: Henry and Debbie Russel

Date visited: _____
Went with: _____
Notes: _____
_____

iew

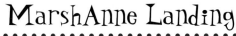

MarshAnne Landing

ciness

www.marshannelanding.com
175 Hogan Road; Oakland; 541.459.8497

k/patio

Hours: Wed–Sun 11:00am-5:00pm (May–Oct);
Sat–Sun 11:00am-5:00pm (Mar–Apr, Nov–Dec)

Tasting Fee: $5.00 for 6-7 tastes

for sale

Wine: 7 varieties; $18.00–22.00
Specializes in food-friendly "out of this world" wines

ic area

Outside: You'll immediately see how there's plenty of room for a flying saucer to land, but this property is only known to have hosted an old stage coach stop. Spacious lawn for summer concerts and events!

us/rv

Inside: Contemporary, big space elevated up high on the hill with a wall of windows so you can enjoy the view. Rotating art gallery, fireplace *and* huge deck!

friendly

Notes: They mixed family names of Marsh and Anne to come up with a play on Martian (MarshAnne). There are a lot of fun names involved in labeling and any coincidences you may find are entirely intentional!

ours

Facts: Established 2001 • 17 acres • Umpqua Valley AVA • 1,200 cases annually

it space

Owners: Greg and Fran Cramer
Winemaker: Greg Cramer

Date visited: _____

Went with: _____

Notes: _____

_____

view

fanciness

deck/patio

food for sale

picnic area

bus/rv

pet friendly

tours

event space

Melrose
. . . .

www.melrosevineyards.com
885 Melqua Road; Roseburg; 541.672.6080

Hours: Daily 11:00am–5:00pm

Tasting Fee: FREE for 3 tastes / $10.00 for 6 tastes
and includes a Melrose glass

Wine: 12 varieties; $12.00–$24.00
Specializes in Pinot Noir, Pinot Gris, and Baco Noir

Outside: You'll be reminded that you really *are* in the
country upon seeing the famous, big ol' brown barn
and miles of vines and pines surrounding you. View
from the patio is especially memorable. Room to roam!

Inside: Cool and cavernous on the inside. Shop the
unique gift boutique with lots of fun wine-related
items. Spend some time on the attached balcony.

Notes: There's something about the place that feels
immediately friendly, happy and fun. It's good times
in the vines. Check website for parties and events.
• Excellent spot for weddings. • The son, Cody, is
becoming a gifted and knowledgeable winemaker!

Facts: Established 1999 • 260 acres (180 producing)
• Umpqua Valley AVA • 3,500 cases annually

Owners: Wayne and Deedy Parker
Winemaker: Cody Parker

Date visited: _____
Went with: _____
Notes: _____
_____

view

ciness

k/patio

for sale

nic area

us/rv

friendly

tours

nt space

Misty Oaks

• •

www.mistyoaksvineyard.com
1310 Misty Oaks Lane; Oakland; 541.459.3558

Hours: Fri–Sun 11:00am-5:00pm (Mem–Thanks);
plus by appointment

Tasting Fee: $4.00 for 6 tastes

Wine: 5 varieties; $10.00–$22.00
Specializes in estate wines

Outside: Take the long, curvy road around and up to
the tasting room at Misty Oaks Vineyard. The house
on the hill has a big lawn and pretty, sprawling views.

Inside: Cozy, small and homey interior with buttercream walls and cushioned wicker chairs. You'll feel
welcomed like a guest in the home of a friend.

Notes: Inquire about some of the stories behind the
wine's fun, meaningful names (i.e. Gobbler's Knob or
Constitution Ridge). • Named for the blanket of fog
that covers the valley in the winter, with only the tops
of the trees peeking out.

Facts: Established 2000 • 15 acres • Umpqua Valley
AVA • 800 cases annually

Owners: Steve and Christy Simmons
Winemakers: Steve and Christy Simmons

Date visited: _____
Went with: _____
Notes: _____

Palotai

view

fanciness

deck/patio

food for sale

picnic area

bus/rv

pet friendly

tours

event space

www.palotaiwines.com
272 Capital Lane; Roseburg; 541.464.0032

Hours: Daily 11:00am-5:00pm (year-round)

Tasting Fee: FREE for 6+ tastes

Wine: 7 varieties; $15.00–$25.00
Specializes in old-world, hand-crafted wines

Outside: Simple home-style barn nestled in the trees. Located right on the banks of the Umpqua River, but you'll need to head 'round back to enjoy the scenery.

Inside: Barrel bar next to barrel room. Dimly lit with low, wooden-beamed ceilings and a somewhat eclectic, European-rustic style.

Notes: Very friendly, relaxed and low-key (i.e. you might hear Bob Marley tunes, but you won't see any little pinky fingers extended here). • Backyard gazebo and patio area coming soon! • Pronounced PAL-o-tie. • Don't miss the "Bull's Blood," a traditional Hungarian wine from the 1500s.

Facts: Established 2002 • 21 acres producing • Umpqua Valley AVA • 1,300 cases annually

Owners: John Olson
Winemaker: Gabor Palotai

Date visited: _____
Went with: _____
Notes: _____
_____

view

ciness

k/patio

for sale

nic area

us/rv

friendly

tours

nt space

Reustle-Prayer Rock

. . . .

www.reustlevineyards.com
960 Cal Henry Road; Roseburg; 541.459.6060

Hours: Tues–Sat 10:00am-5:00pm (year-round)

Tasting Fee: $10.00 for 4 tastes (includes three food pairings / appetizer courses)

Wine: 12 varieties; $19.00–32.00
Specializes in having many award-winning wines including a Grüner Veltliner

Outside: The "Wow!" factor starts with the drive in and doesn't stop until you leave. There really is a peaceful presence in the beautiful, natural surroundings. Picnic on one of two patios or up at one of two rocks.

Inside: Absolutley glorious decor! This place rocks!

Notes: Their four-year-old son coined the named "Prayer Rock" in reference to where he and Dad liked to play and pray. • They are all about making people comfortable and are very hospitality-focused ("Come as Strangers, Leave as Friends" is their tagline).
• Plan on at least an hour for short tour and tastings.

Facts: Established 2001 •200 acres (35 producing)
• Umpqua Valley AVA • 6,000 cases annually

Owners: Stephen and Gloria Reustle
Winemaker: Stephen Reustle

Date visited: _____

Went with: _____

Notes: _____

_____

view

fanciness

deck/patio

food for sale

picnic area

bus/rv

pet friendly

tours

event space

River's Edge Winery

www.riversedgewinery.com
1395 River Drive; Elkton; 541.584.2357

Hours: Daily 11:00am-5:00pm (summer);
Thur–Sun 11:00am-5:00pm (off-season)

Tasting Fee: FREE for 6-7 tastes

Wine: 6-7 varieties; $12.00–$28.00
Specializes in Pinot Noir

Outside: Pretty drive in to the river's edge and easy access off Hwy. 38 on the way back from the coast. Needs better outdoor seating, but a picnic area is being worked on and should be in full bloom for 2010.

Inside: Bare-bones barrels as tasting tables, but with a huge window for river watching.

Notes: Solar-powered with 36 rooftop panels. Follow sustainable farming practices and LIVE guidelines.

Facts: Established 1998 (1972 plantings) • 12 acres • Umpqua Valley AVA • 3,600 cases annually

Owners: Michael and Vonnie Landt
Winemakers: Michael and Vonnie Landt

Date visited: _____
Went with: _____
Notes: _____
_____

Sienna Ridge Estate

● ●

www.siennaridgeestate.com
1876 John Long Road; Oakland; 541.849.3300

Hours: Daily 12:00pmam-6:00pm (year-round)

Tasting Fee: $5.00 for 5 tastes; $10.00 full flight

Wine: 12 varieties; $15.00–$28.00
Specializes in Pinot Noir

Outside: Renovated farmhouse with wrap-around porch and a big side deck. Huge, flat front lawn hosts an antique barn assembled without the use of nails.

Inside: Classic, historic interior with thick crown moldings, paneled windows, and wood floors. It has a nice living room or dining room effect.

Notes: Sienna Ridge is the stand-alone, sole vineyard that makes up the Red Hill Douglas County AVA.
• Tasting room building is the 1908 homestead of Robert Long who had it built for his mother. • Also carries the Domaine de le Rasmus label.

Facts: Established 2003 (1989 plantings) • 500 acres (267 producing) • Red Hill Douglas County AVA
• 2,000 cases annually

Owner: Wayne Hitchings
Winemaker: Terry Brandborg

Date visited: _____
Went with: _____
Notes: _____
_____

view

fanciness

deck/patio

food for sale

picnic area

bus/rv

pet friendly

tours

event space

Spangler
● ●

www.spanglervineyards.com
491 Winery Lane; Roseburg; 541.679.9654

Hours: Daily 11:00am-5:00pm (year-round)

Tasting Fee: FREE for 3 tastes; $5.00 for 5 more

Wine: 14 varieties; $14.00–$30.00
Specializes in Bordeaux varietals

Outside: From Hwy. 5, take the *second* left, about 100 yards past the first stoplight (left-hand turn lane). You, your dogs, or kids can run wild on the giant, sprawling, front yard with wonderful outdoor deck.

Inside: Northwest, ski-lodge-like interior with dark woods everywhere, hand-built stone wall, thick beams, and super-tall slatted windows. Some deli snacks available some times, and gift items too.

Notes: Spangler wines have won a ton of awards – be sure to get details! ● They dry farm, and are considered to be in a "banana belt." It can get pretty dang hot here on a sunny summer day!

Facts: Established 2004 ● 18 acres (5 producing; late 60's plantings) ● Umpqua Valley AVA ● 3,000 cases

Owners: Pat and Loree Spangler
Winemaker: Pat Spangler

Date visited: _____
Went with: _____
Notes: _____
_____

Wild Rose
•••••••••••••••••••••••••••••

www.wildrosevineyard.com
375 Porter Creek Road; Winston; 541.580.5488

Hours: Daily 11:00am-5:00pm (year-round)

Tasting Fee: FREE for 5-6 tastes

Wine: 10 varieties; $20.00–$30.00
Specializes in Pinot Gris and Merlot

Outside: Simple grounds with a few picnic tables scattered about. At first glance, it's a bit farm-barny, but there's some nice nature action taking place down at creekside. Bring a picnic!

Inside: Simple basement tasting room decorated with hanging wire grids of wine-themed art (some by the owners' daughter).

Notes: It's a small place, so you might need to ring the bell for service (or knock at the house next door). • Organically grown grapes with no pesticides. Dry farmed and LIVE certified. • Wild roses used to grow rampant on property, but were ripped out and now just decorate the vines here and there.

Facts: Established 2002 (1995 plantings) • 18 acres • Umpqua Valley AVA • 500 cases annually

Owners: Denise and Carlos Figueroa
Winemakers: Dean Dionestes and Scott Henry IV

Date visited: _____

Went with: _____

Notes: _____

_____

179

Sidebar icons:
view
ciness
k/patio
for sale
nic area
us/rv
friendly
tours
nt space

Rogue/Applegate Valley

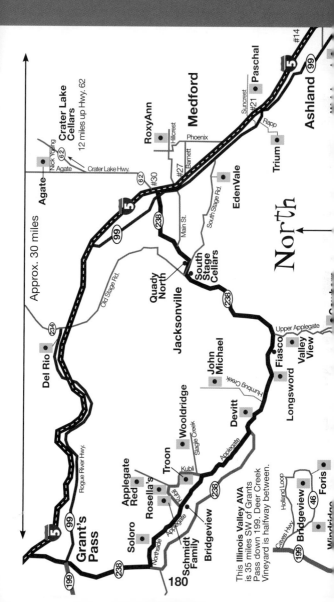

North

Approx. 30 miles

Crater Lake Cellars
12 miles up Hwy. 62

Medford

Ashland

Agate

Crater Lake Hwy.

RoxyAnn

Phoenix

Paschal

Trium

EdenVale

South Stage Cellars

Quady North

Jacksonville

Del Rio

John Michael

Fiasco

Valley View

Upper Applegate

Longsword

Wooldridge

Devitt

Applegate Red

Troon

Rosella's

Kubli

Schmidt Family

Bridgeview

Soloro

Grant's Pass

Bridgeview

Foris

This Illinois Valley AVA
is 35 miles SW of Grants
Pass down 199. Deer Creek
Vineyard is halfway between.

180

view

nciness

ck/patio

d for sale

cnic area

bus/rv

t friendly

tours

ent space

Agate Ridge

● ●

www.agateridgevineyard.com
1098 Nick Young Road; Eagle Point; 541.830.3050

Hours: Tues-Mon 11:00am-5:00pm (year-round); closed January

Tasting Fee: $5.00 flight of 6 tastes

Wine: 12-14 varieties; $13.00-$24.00
Specializes in Petit Syrah and Viognier

Outside: Views in every direction, including a gorgeous wide-open vista of Mt. McLaughlin. Take it in and take your pick of lounging venues with romantic two-seater benches, porch sitting, small or big tables, or sprawl out on a picnic blanket on the extra-large lawn.

Inside: Located inside a refurbished, old farmhouse with several parlors available to sit and sip in a comfy, cozy, country environment.

Notes: Vineyard gets its name from the abundance of agate gemstone found on the property (turned into beautiful jewelry for sale there by a local artist).
• Check their website calendar for summer concerts.

Facts: Established 2005 • 126 acres (30 planted)
• Rogue Valley AVA • 2,700 cases annually

Owners: The Kinderman Family
Winemaker: B. Kiley Evans

Date visited: _____
Went with: _____
Notes: _____
_____

view

fanciness

deck/patio

food for sale

picnic area

bus/rv

pet friendly

tours

event space

Applegate Red

● ●

www.applegatered.com
222 Missouri Flat Road; Grants Pass; 541.450.1072

Hours: Wed–Mon12:00pm–6:00pm (summer);
Sat–Sun11:00am-5:00pm (Sep–May);

Tasting Fee: FREE flight of 3 tastes

Wine: 12 varieties; $28.00-$32.00
Specializes in reds (It's in the name – and the house!)

Outside: It's not every day you see teeny-tiny Sicilian donkeys, but they'll greet you on your way in and set a fun, somewhat quirky tone for the rest of your visit to this bright red farm. It's off the beaten path in the country and a bit off-beat, with some Hawaiian fun thrown in for good measure.

Inside: Very basic inside with a few gifts and some art. Have your tasting out on the porch if possible!

Notes: Be sure to read all the hand-painted signs as there's some good ones. • Check out the party pad perched over the pond with nearby parakeets too. • Feel free to wander and explore the property.

Facts: Established 2007 • 75 acres (16 planted) • Applegate Valley AVA • 1,200 cases annually

Owner: Paul Ferreira
Winemaker: Bryan Wilson

Date visited: _____
Went with: _____
Notes: _____
_____

view

nciness

ck/patio

d for sale

cnic area

ous/rv

t friendly

tours

ent space

Bridgeview

• •

www.bridgeviewwine.com
4210 Holland Loop Road; Cave Junction; 541.592.4688

Hours: Daily 11:00am–5:00pm (year-round)

Tasting Fee: FREE flight of 6+ tastes

Wine: 30 varieties; $8.00-$30.00
Specializes in variety and German-style

Outside: A multi-level fountain impresses you at the entrance and the water showcasing continues with a small, refreshing lake hosting a floating party room! Picnic on the lawn or grab a table on their big deck. Here, you'll get both bridge and mountain views.

Inside: Traditional and simple decor with an extra-long tasting bar and pink walls. The flagship "blue moon" makes appearances in sunlit bottles.

Notes: Many visitors opt to overnight at Bridgeview's B&B, The Kerbyville Inn, with five wine-themed suites.
• Bridgeview also has a second tasting room in Applegate in a can't-miss big red barn (16995 North Applegate Road; Grants Pass; 541.846.1039)

Facts: Established 1986 (1979 plantings) • 370 acres
• Illinois and Applegate Valley AVAs • 80,000 cases

Owners: Robert and Lelo Kerivan
Winemaker: René Eichmann

Date visited: _____
Went with: _____
Notes: _____
_____

Cowhorn

• •

view

fanciness

deck/patio

food for sale

picnic area

bus/rv

pet friendly

tours

event space

www.cowhornwine.com
1665 Eastside Road; Jacksonville; 541.899.6876

Hours: Fri–Mon 11:00am–4:00pm (May1–Labor Day)

Tasting Fee: $5.00 flight of 4-5 tastes

Wine: 4-5 varieties; $18.00-$32.00
Specializes in biodynamic processes

Outside: It's a spectacularly beautiful drive out to this off-the-beaten-path gem nestled peacefully in the surrounding valley. Cowhorn is all about respect for the land and you can feel the positive energy radiate all throughout the open fields, rustling leaves, forested hills and even in the small lake right on the grounds.

Inside: Rather than your typical stand-up tasting bar, there are comfy couches to relax in. Serenity now!

Notes: Totally dedicated to full-throttle biodynamic, holistic, ecologically sustainable and organic farming practices (Demeter USA Verified) • 100% estate grapes used and cared for. • Very "Oregon-y" here.

Facts: Established 2008 • 117 acres (11 producing) • Applegate Valley AVA • 1,600 cases annually

Owners: Bill and Barbara Steele
Winemakers: The Grapes! (with assistance from Bill and friends)

Date visited: _____
Went with: _____
Notes: _____
_____

view

nciness

ck/patio

d for sale

cnic area

bus/rv

t friendly

tours

ent space

Deer Creek

● ●

www.deercreekvineyards.com
2680 Deer Creek Road; Selma; 541.597.4226

Hours: Daily 11:00am–5:00pm (year-round)

Tasting Fee: FREE flight of 3 tastes

Wine: 3 varieties; $14.00-$19.00
Specializes in Chardonnay, Pinot Gris and Pinot Noir

Outside: Easy access from Hwy. 199, clearly marked
by blue signs, and positioned right on Deer Creek
Road. The porch has a stellar view of the Graybacks
and other surrounding mountains.

Inside: New, clean, bright and white tasting room
with soaring cathedral ceilings and two tasting bars.
Good pit stop for both gifts and sips.

Notes: Named for its location real near Deer Creek.
• May reappear soon under different name, as the
Garnetts are ready to retire to Arizona at the time
of this writing. Anyone want a winery?!

Facts: Established 2002 (1991 plantings) • 40 acres
• Illinois Valley AVA • 200 cases annually

Owners: Gary and Ann Garnett
Winemaker: Bryan Wilson

Date visited: _____

Went with: _____

Notes: _____

_____

view

fanciness

deck/patio

food for sale

picnic area

bus/rv

pet friendly

tours

event space

Del Rio Vineyards

www.delriovineyards.com
520 N River Road; Gold Hill; 541.855.2062

Hours: Daily 11:00am-5:00pm (year-round);
Summer hours until 6:00pm

Tasting Fee: $5.00 flight of 6 tastes (one free taste)

Wine: 10 varieties; $15.00-$35.00
Specializes in variety and quality grapes

Outside: Located right off Hwy. 234, you'll easily
spot the big, red, historic Del Rio Orchard packing
house (now winery). The tasting room is over in the
quaint Colonial home. Nice porch and picnic space!

Inside: Take a step back in time in this historic homestead. Neutral tones, natural wood, open space and
comfy couches all contribute to your relaxation.

Notes: Over 200,000 vines producing diverse grape
varieties (they sell a lot to other vineyards). • Their
motto: "Great grapes. Great wines. Great times."
• Del Rio named after being "on the river."

Facts: Established 2001 • 205 acres (15 varietals)
• Rogue Valley AVA • 5,000 cases annually

Owners: Lee and Margaret Traynham; Rob and Jolee
Wallace
Winemaker: Jean-Michel Jussiaume

Date visited: _____
Went with: _____
Notes: _____
_____

186

view

nciness

ck/patio

d for sale

cnic area

bus/rv

t friendly

tours

ent space

Devitt

• •

www.devittwinery.com
11412 Highway 238; Jacksonville; 541.899.7511

Hours: Daily 11:00am-5:00pm (year-round); Best to call ahead and confirm as they are a small place

Tasting Fee: $5.00 flight of 7 tastes

Wine: 13 varieties; $12.00-$30.00
Specializes in boutique estate reds

Outside: Easy access off the main road Hwy. 238 and right in the middle of the Applegate area. Sitting outside at the picnic table is a relaxing and mellow experience, almost like you're in a friend's backyard.

Inside: Cozy tasting bar where you can hunt for flying pigs as you taste! Small and simple but sweet.

Notes: Ask about the flying pigs you'll see every-where! • Pronounced DEV-it and is a family affair.

Facts: Established 2003 • 15 acres (plus sourced local grapes) • Applegate Valley AVA • 2,000 cases

Owners: Jim and Sue Devitt
Winemaker: Jim Devitt

Date visited: _____
Went with: _____
Notes: _____
_____

view

fanciness

deck/patio

food for sale

picnic area

bus/rv

pet friendly

tours

event space

EdenVale

• •

www.edenvalewines.com
2310 Voorhies Road; Medford; 541.512.2955

Hours: Mon–Sat 11:00am-6:00pm and
Sun 12:00pm–4:00pm (year-round)

Tasting Fee: FREE flight of 3 tastes; Reserve flights
$5.00 for 3 tastes or $10.00 for 10 tastes

Wine: 16-18 varieties; $14.00-$35.00
Specializes in "big full-bodied reds and luscious whites"

Outside: Beautiful and historic setting with EdenVale
Pear Orchards and Voorhies mansion. Enjoy the
scenery from an outside patio table or picnic blanket.
Take a walk around the garden and see the playhouse.

Inside: High-end simplicity with dark cabinetry.

Notes: They like providing a wine education experience.
• They also own Enoteca Wine Library in downtown
Ashland (17 N. Main; 503.482.3377 Tues–Sat 11–8).
• They like to experiment a bit. • Summertime Thursday
Night Jazz in the Gardens. • Weekend winery tours
and barrel sampling at 12:00pm and 2:00 pm.

Facts: Established 1999 • 27 acres (plus sourced
S. Oregon grapes) • Rogue Valley AVA • 10,000 cases

Owner: Anne Root (Fourth generation Root Family)
Winemaker: Ashley Campanella

Date visited: _____
Went with: _____
Notes: _____
_____

view

nciness

ck/patio

d for sale

nic area

Fiasco Winery

www.fiascowinery.com
8035 Hwy 238; Jacksonville; 541.899-9645

Hours: Wed–Mon 11:00am-6:00pm (year-round);
Closed in January

Tasting Fee: $5.00 flight of 6+ tastes

Wine: 10 varieties; $19.00-$36.00
Specializes in Zinfandel and other reds

Outside: Head right to the picnic space located
behind the tasting room building if you want a view!

Inside: Big, open room with many little, unique design
touches. Lots of tables and views to the outside.

Notes: The winery is actually not on-site (their other
label is Jacksonville Vineyards, and is located just up
the road on the other side). They still do events over
at the Jacksonville location, but this place is the one
tasting room for both. All wines are 100% estate.
• The word "Fiasco" has several meanings: Italian
for theatrical, or to make a bottle, or might refer to
a straw Chianti holder.

Facts: Established 1999 • 18 acres (producing)
• Applegate Valley AVA • 3,000 cases

Owners: David and Pam Palmer
Winemaker: David Palmer

Date visited: _____

Went with: _____

Notes: _____

_____

view

fanciness

deck/patio

food for sale

picnic area

bus/rv

pet friendly

tours

event space

Foris

• •

www.foriswine.com
654 Kendall Road; Cave Junction; 800.843.6747

Hours: Daily 11:00am–5:00pm (year-round)

Tasting Fee: FREE flight of 6+ tastes

Wine: 20 varieties; $13.00-$20.00
Specializes in Pinot Noir

Outside: Take the winding, one-lane road about a mile off the Holland Loop (marked by signs). This tree-lined, curvy drive will bring you to sprawling views! Enclosed, peaceful little backyard too.

Inside: They didn't go too crazy with décor here. The tasting room inside the stone-front building is low-key and understated with green walls and low lights.

Notes: As their website explains, "Foris" is Latin for "out of doors," and thus conveys the mood of the flowing rivers and lush, fir-covered Siskiyou Mountains which surround the vineyards. • Family-owned and family-managed winery whose collective goal is to keep everybody involved in the business happy.

Facts: Established 1986 • 140 acres • Illinois Valley AVA • 25,000 cases annually

Owner: Ted Gerber
Winemaker: Bryan Wilson

Date visited: _____
Went with: _____
Notes: _____

view

ncinesss

ck/patio

d for sale

cnic area

bus/rv

t friendly

tours

ent space

Longsword

• •

www.longswordvineyard.com
8555 Highway 238; Jacksonville; 541.899.1746

Hours: Daily 12:00pm–5:00pm (year-round);
By appointment in February

Tasting Fee: FREE flight of 5-6 tastes

Wine: 5 varieties; $18.00-$28.00
Specializes in Frizzante-style Chardonnay

Outside: Gorgeous scenery with distant mountains surrounding you in this flat, peaceful valley. You can watch paragliders!

Inside: Brand new tasting room tastefully done in Pottery Barn style. Sliding glass doors line the wall so the view never stops. Enjoy being served with tastings done at café tables inside or out rather than at a bar.

Notes: Music on weekends all summer long. • Label name comes from wife's last name (Spanish translation means "long sword").

Facts: Established 2002 • 18 acres (1982 plantings, plus local sourced grapes) • Applegate Valley AVA • 1,500 cases annually

Owners: Matthew Sorensen and Maria Largaespada
Winemaker: Matthew Sorensen

Date visited: _____

Went with: _____

Notes: _____

_____

Paschal

• •

view

fanciness

deck/patio

food for sale

picnic area

bus/rv

pet friendly

tours

event space

www.paschalwinery.com
1122 Suncrest Road; Talent; 541.535.7957

Hours: Daily 11:00am–6:00pm (year-round)

Tasting Fee: Two FREE tastes; $5.00 flight of 6+

Wine: 12 varieties; $20.00-$35.00
Specializes in unique blends and Syrah

Outside: Easy to find and hard to leave. It looks a lot like Tuscany both inside and out. Take a walk around the swan lake out front or just sit and admire it from the veranda. Spectacular views!

Inside: It's a stunning entrance into the huge tasting room with golden stucco walls, several seating areas and gallery art demanding attention. Arched paneled windows bring the outside in. Spectacular interior!

Notes: Some fun events hosted here—check the calendar. And join the wine club! • Gallery art rotates every couple months with work from very talented local artists. • *Ashland Daily* voted Paschal the "best winery to visit in the Rogue Valley."

Facts: Established 2001 (1989 plantings) · 8 acres (planted) · Rogue Valley AVA • 3,000 cases annually

Owners: Roy and Jill Paschal
Winemaker: Joe Dobbes

Date visited: _____

Went with: _____

Notes: _____

_____

Rosella's

•••••••••••••••••••••••••••••••

www.rosellasvineyard.com
184 Missouri Flat Road; Grants Pass; 541.846.6372

Hours: Thur–Mon 11:00am-5:00pm (year-round)

Tasting Fee: FREE flight of 4-6 tastes

Wine: 6 varieties; $16.00-$20.00
Specializes in reds (Cabernet and Mer-Zin)

Outside: An easy skip off the road to include in the North Applegate line-up. It's back to the simple life with a home, home on the range—within very close range of the tasting room and the barn-style winery.

Inside: Owner-operated, bare-bones-basic tasting room with some nice photography and wooden placards adorning walls.

Notes: Named after owner's late mother, Rosella.
• The wine label was designed around an original oil painting done by local artist Morgan Johnson.
• Several other artist's wares for sale and display.

Facts: Established 2004 • 8 acres • Applegate Valley AVA • 800 cases annually

Owners: Rex and Sandi Garouette
Winemaker: Rex Garouette

Date visited: _____
Went with: _____
Notes: _____
_____

Photos by Michael Davis

2007
ROXYANN
Pinot gris

view

fanciness

deck/patio

food for sale

picnic area

bus/rv

pet friendly

tours

event space

RoxyAnn

www.roxyann.com
3285 Hillcrest Road; Medford; 541.776.2315

Hours: Daily 11:00am-6:00pm (year-round)

Tasting Fee: $3.00–$5.00 for 3-7 tastes

Wine: 24 varieties; $16.50–$42.00
Specializes in big red varietals and blends

Outside: Country farm charm with all-too-easy access from Hwy. 5. Beautiful gardens with tables and tents overlook the nearby vineyard and orchard.

Inside: Big yet very welcoming tasting room with a homey and warm vibe. Gift shop, deli case, beer, and local fresh produce for sale.

Notes: LIVE and Salmon-Safe sustainable vineyard management. • RoxyAnn is taken from "Roxy Ann Peak," a large geologic feature in the Rogue Valley. The vineyards are on its southwest slopes. • Wines from several neighbors sold too. • Summer farmers market adds to country-store feel (Wed & Fri).

Facts: Established 2002 • 75 acres (plus sources grapes from other Rogue Valley vineyards) • Rogue Valley AVA • 15,000 cases annually

Owners: The Day-Parsons family
Winemaker: John Quinones

Date visited: _____
Went with: _____
Notes: _____
_____

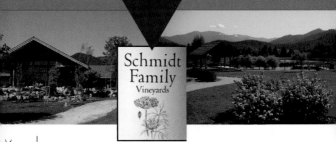

view

nciness

ck/patio

d for sale

nic area

ous/rv

friendly

tours

nt space

Schmidt Family Vineyards

• •

www.sfvineyards.com
330 Kubli Road; Grants Pass; 541.846.9985

Hours: Daily 12:00pm-6:00pm (May 1–Dec 1);
Fri–Sun 12–5:00pm (Winter)

Tasting Fee: FREE for one taste; $3.00 flight of 3
tastes; $5.00 flight of 5 tastes

Wine: 5 varieties; $18.00-$30.00
Specializes in Cabernet Sauvignon and Syrah

Outside: Spectacular! Stunning! This place has it all—
a small lake with a long pier, super-cute gazebo,
Adirondack chairs, and swings. And that's just in the
front. Out back, there's also a gorgeously landscaped
wine garden area with beautiful views too.

Inside: *Architectural Digest*-worthy Northwest style!
Gorgeous cabinetry behind tasting bar (the owner
also has a cabinetry business (Northwestern Design).
Aesthetic attention to detail (and wood) everywhere
you look. It's all just so… marvelous!

Notes: I literally cannot say enough (no more room).

Facts: Established 2004 • 28 acres • Applegate
Valley AVA • 2,700 cases annually

Owners: Cal and Judy Schmidt
Winemaker: Cal Schmidt

Date visited: _____
Went with: _____
Notes: _____
_____

view

fanciness

deck/patio

food for sale

picnic area

bus/rv

pet friendly

tours

event space

Soloro

• •

no website yet
9110 N. Applegate Road; Grants Pass; 541.862.2693

Hours: Sat–Sun 1:00pm-5:00pm (April–Dec 10);
closed Dec–March

Tasting Fee: FREE for 3 tastes

Wine: 3-5 varieties; $18.00–$24.00
Specializes in Rhone varietals

Outside: Head up the gravel road to the top of the
hill to find Soloro's brand-new tasting room set up in
a nice manufactured home. Outside deck for relaxing.

Inside: Decorated in warm, gold tones to reflect the
name. Simple, friendly, living-room style space.

Notes: The owners show their Spanish heritage
through using colors from the Spanish flag and in
the Soloro name, which translates to "sun gold."

Facts: Established 2005 • 5 acres (under vine)
• Applegate Valley AVA • 300 cases annually

Owners: Tim and June Navarro
Winemakers: Linda Donovan and Steve Anderson

Date visited: _____

Went with: _____

Notes: _____

_____

view

...ciness

...ck/patio

...l for sale

...nic area

...us/rv

... friendly

tours

...nt space

Trium Wines
• •

www.triumwines.com
7112 Rapp Lane; Talent; 541.535.6093

Hours: Thurs–Mon 11:00am–5:30pm (Apr–Sep);
by appointment off-season

Tasting Fee: $5.00 for 4-5 tastes

Wine: 5 varieties; $19.00–$38.00
Specializes in highlighting Southern Oregon grapes

Outside: Go up the hill from the turn, and turn to go
up another hill, to find this delightful hidden gem with
fantastic views and a couple of sweet porch areas.

Inside: The little house here hosts a little tasting
room inside. Find your favorite wine for your picnic
outside! Very peaceful, small, and beautiful.

Notes: Trium (TREE-um) is Latin for "of the three."
The three are vineyards in the Rogue Valley Appellation.
"Of the three" is also a reference to their first Cuvee
(blend) which mixed three reds. • LIVE certified.

Facts: Established 2001 (1990 plantings) • 35 acres
• Rogue Valley AVA • 1,000 cases annually

Owners: Nancy Tappan / Kurt and Laura Lotspeich
Winemakers: Peter Rosback and Aron Hess

Date visited: _____
Went with: _____
Notes: _____

Troon

view

fanciness

deck/patio

food for sale

picnic area

bus/rv

pet friendly

tours

event space

www.troonvineyard.com
1475 Kubli Road; Grants Pass; 541.846.9900

Hours: Daily 11:00am–5:00pm (year-round);
Sat–Sun 11:00am–5:00pm in January

Tasting Fee: $5.00 for 5 tastes; try the weekend
"Vino Lab" with $15.00 outside seated food pairings

Wine: 25 varieties; $18.00–$25.00
Specializes in Cab, Zinfandel and blends

Outside: Obviously gorgeous from the entrance on in.
Back patio embraces you with abundant lushness!

Inside: The elegance of the Tuscan exterior continues
inside with giant windows overlooking old vines, green
forested hills and seasonal snowcapped mountains.

Notes: They take a natural approach to wine making
and use sustainable farming methods. • Open until
6:00pm in the summer. • Unique "Vermentino White."
• Second tasting room in downtown Carlton.

Facts: Established 2003 (1972 plantings) • 100 acres
(33 planted plus sourced grapes) • Applegate Valley
AVA • 7,500 cases annually

Owners: The Martin Family (originally established
by Dick Troon)
Winemaker: Herb Quady

Date visited: _____
Went with: _____
Notes: _____

Valley View

view

nciness

ck/patio

d for sale

cnic area

bus/rv

et friendly

tours

ent space

www.valleyviewwinery.com
1000 Upper Applegate Rd; Jacksonville; 541.899.8468

Hours: Daily 11:00am–5:00pm (year-round)

Tasting Fee: $5.00 for 6+ tastes

Wine: Valley View: 3-4 varieties; $12.00–$14.00
Anna Maria Reserve Label: 9 varieties; $18.00–$35.00
Specializes in Viognier and Tempranillo

Outside: Right off the road (but relatively low traffic noise). Gorgeous views from front porch and any of many tables. Down in the valley rather than up high.

Inside: Spacious and gallery-like, open and bright white space. The oversized, circular bar provides lots of room for tasting and making new friends. Giant front windows provide extra light and valley views.

Notes: Valley View was originally founded by Peter Britt in the 1850's. Years after his death in 1906, Valley View was the first local start-up since prohibition.

Facts: Established 1976 (1971 plantings) • 27 acres (plus sourced local grapes) • Applegate Valley AVA • 9,000+ cases annually

Owners: The Wisnovski Family (originally established by Anna Marie Wisnovski)
Winemaker: John Guerrero

Date visited: _____

Went with: _____

Notes: _____

_____

Weisingers of Ashland

view

fanciness

deck/patio

food for sale

picnic area

bus/rv

pet friendly

tours

event space

www.weisingers.com
3150 Siskiyou Boulevard; Ashland; 541.488.5989

Hours: Sun–Thur 11:00am-5:00pm ('til 7:00pm Fri–Sat) (May–Nov); Wed–Sun 11:00am–5:00pm (winter)

Tasting Fee: One FREE taste and/or: $3.00 flight of white wines; $7.00 reds only; $8.00 for the full flight

Wine: 16-20 varieties; $14.00–$28.00
Specializes in blends

Outside: Positioned high on a hill and just 14 miles from the California border, you can see forever here! Wide open spaces viewed from above via a triple-tiered deck, or looking out the giant windows.

Inside: Modern and welcoming, somewhat German interior with a long, black marble, L-shaped bar.

Notes: On the right day, you may just find it very difficult to leave, and you may not have to—there's a guest cottage hideaway here (see website).
• Weisingers opens early and goes late on weekends and is easy to find via the blue roadside signage.

Facts: Established 1988 (1979 plantings) • 8 acres (planted) • Rogue Valley AVA • 3,000 cases annually

Owner: John Weisinger
Winemaker: Eric Weisinger

Date visited: _____

Went with: _____

Notes: _____

_____

view

nciness

eck/patio

d for sale

cnic area

bus/rv

et friendly

tours

ent space

Windridge

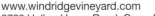

www.windridgevineyard.com
2789 Holland Loop Road; Cave Junction; 541.592.5333

Hours: Wed–Sun 11:00am–5:00pm (Apr–Oct);
By Appt. Nov–Mar

Tasting Fee: FREE for 2 tastes

Wine: 2 varieties; $22.00–$26.00
Specializes in Pinot Noir and Viognier

Outside: Slow down your pace at this cute little
place! Peaceful homestyle ranch set in the middle of
the valley and surrounded by mountains on all sides.
Nice, relaxing back garden area with horsies!

Inside: Very simple enclosed porch with big windows
so you don't miss the vista. Tiny tasting table is all
that's needed for tiny, tasty tasting.

Notes: Name on wine label is Bendock Estate. • Winery
is located on old Fort Briggs property (area settled in
1864) and is the site of an old race track with several
Kentucky Derby winners buried on the grounds.
• Walking and hiking trails. Creekside access.

Facts: Established 2003 (1989 plantings) • 50 acres
(8 planted) • Illinois Valley AVA • 200 cases annually

Owners: Cate and Terry Bendock
Winemaker: Terry Bendock

Date visited: _____
Went with: _____
Notes: _____
_____

view

fanciness

deck/patio

food for sale

picnic area

bus/rv

pet friendly

tours

event space

Wooldridge Creek

• •

www.wcwinery.com
818 Slagle Creek Road; Grants Pass; 541.846.6364

Hours: Sat–Sun 11:00am–5:00pm (year-round);
By appt. other days

Tasting Fee: $5.00 for 4 tastes (two free)

Wine: 10-12 varieties; $24.00–$36.00
Specializes in European-style and unique blends

Outside: Beautiful views of the Siskiyous! Very nice lawn area with tables and lounge chairs. Keep your eyes peeled for local critters – and bears!

Inside: Upscale, NW-style tasting room with fireplace inside, and a second tasting area outside (that looks like an inside with comfy couches and pillows).

Notes: They have established weekend hours, but they are always around, so call on weekdays and someone should be there. • Named for family who settled here.
• Sustainable and certified LIVE winery and vineyard.

Facts: Established 2003 (1976 plantings) • 58 acres of grapes • Applegate Valley AVA • 4,000 cases

Owners: Mary and Ted Warrick / Kara Olmo / Greg Paneitz
Winemakers: Kara Olmo and Greg Paneitz

Date visited: _____

Went with: _____

Notes: _____

_____

Area Tasting Rooms

Crater Lake Cellars
www.craterlakecellars.com
21882 Hwy 62; Shady Cove; 541.878.4200
Hours: Thur–Mon 11:00am-5:30pm (May-Dec);
Thurs-Sat 11:00am-5:00pm (Jan-Apr but call ahead)
Tasting Fee: FREE for 6+ tastes
Wine: 20 varieties; $8.00–$19.00
Located behind the 76 gas station off the highway on the way to Crater Lake. Lots of variety and value. Stock up!

John Michael Champagne Cellars
no website yet
1425 Humbug Creek Road; Jacksonville; 541.846.0810
Hours: Fri-Sun 11:00am-5:00pm (May-Dec; closed Jan-Apr)
Tasting Fee: $5.00 for 6+ tastes
Wine: 10 varieties; $12.00–$25.00
Head here for champagnes and still wines. Ultra-casual. Be sure to ask to see Mongo!

Quady North
www.quadynorth.com
255 California Street; Jacksonville; 541.702.2123
Hours: Wed-Mon 12:30pm-6:30pm (summer);
Thur-Mon 12:30pm-5:30pm (off-season)
Tasting Fee: $5.00 for 5 tastes
Wine: 4 varieties; $12.50–$35.00
Cool space in super-quaint, downtown Jacksonville. Labels are well-designed and resemble tattoo art.

South Stage Cellars
www.southstagecellars.com
125 S. Third Street; Jacksonville; 541.899.9120
Hours: Daily 11:00am-7:00pm; Fri 'til 9:00pm (year-round)
Tasting Fee: $5.00 for 5 tastes
Wine: 7 varieties; $18.00-$27.00
Super-quaint space in cool, historic building in Jacksonville. Join in on Friday local's night! Check out other OR wines too.

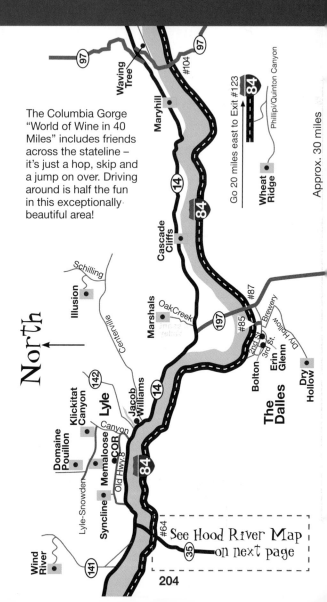

The Columbia Gorge "World of Wine in 40 Miles" includes friends across the stateline – it's just a hop, skip and a jump on over. Driving around is half the fun in this exceptionally beautiful area!

Go 20 miles east to Exit #123

Approx. 30 miles

Phillipi/Quinton Canyon

Waving Tree

Maryhill

Wheat Ridge

Cascade Cliffs

Schilling

Illusion

Centerville

Marshals

OakCreek

Brewery

Dry Hollow

Bolton

Erin Glenn

The Dalles

North

Klickitat Canyon

Lyle

Jacob Williams

Domaine Pouillon

Canyon

COR

Syncline

Memaloose

Old Hwy 8

Lyle-Snowden

Wind River

See Hood River Map on next page

204

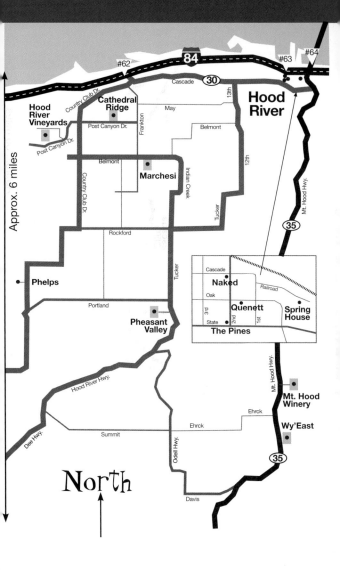

84

#62   #63   #64

Cascade **30**

Country Club Dr.   13th

Hood River

Hood River Vineyards

Cathedral Ridge   May

Post Canyon Dr.   Frankton

Belmont

Belmont

12th

Post Canyon Dr.

Approx. 6 miles

Belmont

Marchesi   Indian Creek

Country Club Dr.

Tucker

35

Mt. Hood Hwy.

Rockford

Tucker

Cascade

Naked

Railroad

Oak

Phelps

Portland

3rd   **Quenett**   **Spring House**

State   2nd   1st

Pheasant Valley   **The Pines**

Mt. Hood Hwy.

Hood River Hwy.

Mt. Hood Winery

Ehrck

Ehrck   **Wy'East**

Summit

Dee Hwy.   Odell Hwy.

35

North

Davis

view

fanciness

deck/patio

food for sale

picnic area

bus/rv

pet friendly

tours

event space

Cascade Cliffs

● ●

www.cascadecliffs.com
8866 Hwy 14; Wishram, WA; 509.767.1100

Hours: Daily 10:00am-6:00pm (year-round)

Tasting Fee: FREE for 6+ tastes

Wine: 7 varieties; $10.00–$35.00
Specializes in Nebbiolo and Barbera

Outside: Located near the river, but no view from tasting room, and limited views from grounds immediately outside. Views of towering desert rocks.

Inside: It's a room of wood with the walls, ceiling and bar all covered in knotty, natural pine. Rustic with mini barrel tables, chalkboard art and friendly wine-istas.

Notes: Label art done in reference to and with reverance for petroglyph symbols from 7,000 years ago. You decide – bull's head or wine vines? • They have the oldest Barbera in Washington.

Facts: Established 1998 • 23 acres (some 1986 plantings) • Columbia Gorge AVA • 4,000 cases

Owners: Bob Lorkowski and family
Winemaker: Bob Lorkowski

Date visited: _____

Went with: _____

Notes: _____

_____

view

anciness

eck/patio

od for sale

cnic area

bus/rv

et friendly

tours

ent space

Cathedral Ridge

• •

www.cathedralridgewinery.com
4200 Post Canyon Road; Hood River; 541.386.2882

Hours: Daily 11:00am-6:00pm (June-Sep);
Daily 11:00am-5:00pm (Oct-May)

Tasting Fee: $5.00 for 4 tastes

Wine: 20 varieties; $15.00-$32.00
Specializes in Syrah and Cabernet

Outside: The park-like setting of Cathedral Ridge welcomes you with a small, tree-lined grove, artsy sculpture pieces, picnic tables, flower beds, and a Papa-Bear-sized bench overlooking the Gorge.

Inside: The first extra-long tasting bar overlooks the grounds, and there are two *more* bars that will open if need be, so no one goes thirsty. It's a party place!

Notes: The winery is named for a rock formation on Mt. Hood called "Cathedral Ridge." • Named "Winery of the Year" in 2007 by Wine Press NW. • They will organize tours for groups and host large events too.

Facts: Established 2003 • 6 acres • Grapes sourced from Columbia Gorge AVA • 4,000 cases annually

Owner: Robb Bell
Winemaker: Michael Sebastiani

Date visited: _____
Went with: _____
Notes: _____
_____

view

fanciness

deck/patio

food for sale

picnic area

bus/rv

pet friendly

tours

event space

COR Cellars
. . . .

www.corcellars.com
151 Old Highway 8; Lyle, WA; 509.365.2744

Hours: Wed–Sun 11:00am-6:00pm (Apr–Nov);
by appointment other times

Tasting Fee: $4.00 for 4-5 tastes

Wine: 4-5 varieties; $14.00–$25.00
Specializes in Alsacian whites and Bordeaux reds

Outside: Not an exceptionally glamourous place
for a picnic or anything. It is a hard-working winery,
without official vineyard, except for "experimental"
plots of on-site vines.

Inside: A small gallery of old poster, original and
vintage art adorns the walls in this small space.
It's all about the wine here.

Notes: They sell lots of wine to Californians. You're
lucky if you live closer! • Tuscany-trained Luke and
his farmer father Adrian meticulously study vine
growth patterns and track the best.

Facts: Established 2004 • Grapes sourced from
Columbia Gorge AVA and Horse Heaven Hills AVA
• 2,200 cases

Owner: Luke Bradford
Winemaker: Luke Bradford

Date visited: _____
Went with: _____
Notes: _____

view

anciness

eck/patio

od for sale

cnic area

bus/rv

et friendly

tours

ent space

Domaine Pouillon

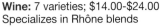

www.domainepouillon.com
170 Lyle-Snowden Road; Lyle, WA; 509.365.2795

Hours: Thur–Sun 11:00am-6:00pm (Mar 1–Nov 1);
Closed Nov–Feb

Tasting Fee: $3.00 for 4-5 tastes

Wine: 7 varieties; $14.00-$24.00
Specializes in Rhône blends

Outside: It's a farmish-rustic entrance that cutens up
once you enter the property through the artisan gate.
Follow the steps down to the tucked-away tasting room.

Inside: Very small but cozy and warm room inside
a barn-like bar area with low ceilings and low light.

Notes: The culinary background of both owners extends
through their hospitality with offerings of breads,
cheeses and chocolates (truffles if you're lucky!)
• Formerly known as Domaine Pierre Noire, now
named after owners' last name. • There are about 50
chickens that work hard to make fresh eggs for sale.

Facts: Established 2006 • 20 acres • Columbia
Gorge AVA (plus sources from other area AVAs
• 1,500 cases annually

Owners: Alexis and Juliet Pouillon
Winemaker: Alexis Pouillon

Date visited: _____
Went with: _____
Notes: _____
_____

view

fanciness

deck/patio

food for sale

picnic area

bus/rv

pet friendly

tours

event space

Dry Hollow

• •

www.dryhollowvineyards.com
3410 Dry Hollow Lane; The Dalles; 541.296.2953

Hours: Saturday 1:00pm-5:00pm (Mem–Thanks)

Tasting Fee: $5.00 for 5-6 tastes

Wine: 6 varieties; $15.00–$26.00
Specializes in Syrah and Merlot

Outside: Follow the twists and turns of Dry Hollow Rd. to find this modern-style cabin located way up high and right in the middle of peaceful cherry orchards and the appropriately named Hi-Valley Vineyard.

Inside: Golden walls with natural wood trim and high ceilings. Two walls of giant windows so you don't miss the outside when you're inside.

Notes: A beautiful destination for a beautiful day!
• Formerly an old dairy farm. • Excellent prices on a absolutely gorgeous event space.

Facts: Established 2003 • 15 acres • Columbia Gorge AVA • 500 cases annually

Owners: Bridget and Eric Nesley
Winemaker: Rich Cushman

Date visited: _____
Went with: _____
Notes: _____

decor

ood for sale

vent space

gift shop

Erin Glenn Winery

• •

www.eringlenn.com
710 East Second Street; The Dalles; 541.296.4707

Hours: Fri–Sun 12:00pm–5:00pm

Tasting Fee: FREE for 4 tastes

Wine: 12 varieties; $13.00–$27.00
Specializes in single vineyard, unique varietals
and eclectic blends

Notes: Commonly referred to as Erin Glenn at the Mint,
this very cool space is *the* place to go in The Dalles!
This ultra-cool, urban winery took over a giant, historic
building downtown that was originally built to be a
U.S. Mint, commissioned by President Abraham
Lincoln in 1864. Lucky for us, the Gold Rush didn't
cooperate with those plans and we now get to enjoy
some great wine here! • Try to hit a Friday night visit,
when they host live music and are open until 9:00pm
(appetizers are available then too). • Erin is the ancient
name for "Ireland," and Glenn is a secret valley.
• They also offer Guinness beer (another nod to Irish
roots) and two rotating Northwest microbrews.

Facts: Established 2003 • Sources grapes throughout
Columbia Valley AVA • 3,000-4,000 cases annually

Owner: Tim Schechtel
Winemaker: Tim Schechtel

Date visited: _____

Went with: _____

Notes: _____

_____

view

fanciness

deck/patio

food for sale

picnic area

bus/rv

pet friendly

tours

event space

Hood River Vineyards

www.hoodrivervineyards.us
4693 Westwood Drive; Hood River; 541.386.3772

Hours: Daily 11:00am–5:00pm (Apr–Oct);
Thurs–Mon (off-season)

Tasting Fee: $5.00 for 6+ tastes

Wine: 8-15 varieties; $12.00–$25.00
Specializes in old-world style reds and Ports

Outside: Winery barn sits near a small grove of trees
with a couple of picnic tables and lots of lawn space.

Inside: Bare-bones and basic interior with smallish
tasting bar, wood stove, and stone wall all located
next to the barrel room. Windows do not provide view.

Notes: The oldest winery in the Gorge got first dibs
on using the Hood River name. • Located along the
"fruit loop" drive, there are several on-site orchards
with pears, apples and cherries. • Ultra-casual and
unpretentious, they are "welcoming to beginners."

Facts: Established 1981 • 70 acres • Columbia
Gorge AVA • 5,000 cases annually

Owners: Bernard and Anne Lerch
Winemaker: Bernard Lerch

Date visited: _____
Went with: _____
Notes: _____
_____

view

winciness

deck/patio

food for sale

picnic area

bus/rv

pet friendly

tours

event space

Illusion

• •

www.illusionwine.com
31 Schilling Road; Lyle, WA; 206.261.1682

Hours: Sat 11:00am–5:00pm; Sun 11:00am–4:00pm
(May–Sep only)

Tasting Fee: FREE for 5-7 tastes

Wine: 7 varieties; $13.00–$19.00
Specializes in Bordeaux blends

Outside: This place is *really* off the beaten path!
And high! Mark your speedometer from Lyle and pay
attention for Schilling Rd. and winery driveway. You'll
enjoy a beautiful 11-mile drive before arriving at this
little home which stands alone with nothing around
for miles. Wildflowers adorn the hillsides. Wildly
winding roads and super windy!

Inside: Simple but nice tasting room with open doors
to the wide open spaces outside.

Notes: Cool label art is especially perfect for their
"Apparition" label, created from an original painting.

Facts: Established 2002 • 1 on-site acre of grapes
(plus sourced area grapes) • Columbia Valley AVA
• 500-700 cases annually

Owners: Dave and Dina Guest
Winemaker: Dave Guest

Date visited: _____
Went with: _____
Notes: _____
_____

view

fanciness

deck/patio

food for sale

picnic area

bus/rv

pet friendly

tours

event space

Klickitat Canyon Winery

www.klickitatcanyonwinery.com
6 Lyle Snowden Road; Lyle; 509.365.2900

Hours: Fri–Sun 12:00pm-6:00pm (summer);
Sat–Sun 12:00pm-6:00pm (off season Apr–Nov)

Tasting Fee: $3.00 for 6+ tastes

Wine: 12–15 varieties; $9.00–$20.00
Specializes in "pure" wines (see Notes below)

Outside: Definitely a working winery. They believe in putting native flora back into the vineyard, and you may see pretty wildflowers and high grasses everywhere.

Inside: As-basic-as-can-be tasting bar with Grateful Dead kind of vibe. Totally casual place with a big front garage filled with mosaic-topped café tables on eclectic carpets and rugs.

Notes: No sulfites added • Vegan • No yeasts added
• There are no residual sugars • Columbia Gorge and varietals are 100% pure. • Certified Organic Processes.
• Inquire about camping, full moon parties and live music.

Facts: Established 1993 • 5 acres (plus sourced from other organically minded vineyards) • Columbia Gorge AVA • 600 cases annually

Owners: The Dobson family
Winemaker: Robin Dobson

Date visited: _____
Went with: _____
Notes: _____
_____

view

anciness

eck/patio

od for sale

icnic area

bus/rv

et friendly

tours

ent space

Marchesi

● ●

www.marchesivineyards.com
3955 Belmont Drive; Hood River; 541.386.1800

Hours: Fri–Sun 11:00am-6:00pm (spring–fall)

Tasting Fee: $1.00 per taste (4-5)

Wine: 5 varieties; $18.00–$28.00
Specializes in Italian varietals

Outside: On relatively flat land, surrounded by vines and a parking lot, lies several buildings with just one being the newly built, stand-alone tasting room/house.

Inside: Simple and homey inside with just a tiny bit of Italy thrown in, this small room with lots of windows and cathedral ceilings keeps you covered in lots of light. Gold walls, furniture and carpet warm it up.

Notes: Talk to the owner, or simply taste the wine itself, and you can tell the Barbera, Dolcetto, Pinot Grigio and Pinot Noir are all grown with passion!

Facts: Established 2006 • 8 acres • Columbia Gorge AVA • 1,500 cases annually

Owner: Franco Marchesi
Winemaker: Alexis Pouillon

Date visited: _____
Went with: _____
Notes: _____
_____

view

fanciness

deck/patio

food for sale

picnic area

bus/rv

pet friendly

tours

event space

Marshal's

● ●

www.marshalsvineyard.com
150 Oak Creek Road; Dallesport, WA; 509.767.4633

Hours: Daily 9:00am–6:00pm (year-round)

Tasting Fee: $5.00 for 6+ tastes

Wine: 12 varieties; $12.00–$25.00
Specializes in Barbera

Outside: Simple, blue, barn-style winery and tasting room building with an old country-store feel.

Inside: Big, open, lofted garage with picnic tables for parties and low-key, very casual atmosphere.

Notes: They have a loyal community following and focus on friendliness and good times. • Deli case with some nibbles – and they've got cold beer too. • Named after their son, Marshal.

Facts: Established 1999 • 31 acres • Columbia Gorge AVA • 4,000 cases annually

Owner: Ron Johnson
Winemaker: Ron Johnson

Date visited: _____
Went with: _____
Notes: _____
_____

view

nciness

ck/patio

d for sale

nic area

ous/rv

: friendly

tours

nt space

Maryhill

• •

www.maryhillwinery.com
9774 Hwy 14; Goldendale, WA; 877.627.9445

Hours: Daily 10:00am–6:00pm (year-round)

Tasting Fee: FREE flight of 6+ tastes;
$5.00 for reserve flight of 4 tastes

Wine: 28 varieties; $12.00–$28.00
Specializes in fruit-forward reds

Outside: You'll have spectacular views in all directions
of the Columbia Gorge, Columbia River, Mt. Hood and
the high desert, so pack a lunch and enjoy the plentiful
seating out on the giant, elevated patio deck!

Inside: The 3,000 sq.ft. tasting room has a beautiful,
antique-style, carved wood bar that can get a bit
crowded, especially now that they were awarded "2009
Washington Winery of theYear" by WinePress NW.

Notes: Maryhill summer concerts are wildly popular.
• Seattle Magazine claims "Best Destination Winery in
Washington." • Originally owned by Sam and Mary Hill.
• Free live music on Saturdays in the summer.

Facts: Established 2001 • 80 on-site acres • Sources
from all over Columbia Valley AVAs • 80,000 cases

Owners: Craig and Vicki Leuthold
Winemaker: Richard Bachelor

Date visited: _____

Went with: _____

Notes: _____

_____

view

fanciness

deck/patio

food for sale

picnic area

bus/rv

pet friendly

tours

event space

Memaloose
• •
McCormick Family Vineyard

www.winesofthegorge.com
101 Lyle-Snowden Road; Lyle, WA; 360.635.2887

Hours: Thurs–Sun 11:00am-5:30pm (Mar.1–Nov.30)

Tasting Fee: $5.00 for 4-5 tastes

Wine: 12 varieties; $12.00–$25.00
Specializes in food wines (dry, low oak)

Outside: Enjoy spectacularly gorgeous views from their site at Mistral Ranch. Perched 1,000 feet above the Columbia River, and facing Mt. Hood head-on, it's hard to beat this view! Even the drive up is great! Perfect place to picnic and/or play bocce ball too.

Inside: Sigh. All this beauty and the tiny tasting room doesn't showcase it. You'll sip at a small tasting table which gets pretty cramped given their popularity.

Notes: There are several islands in the Columbia River named Memaloose, which is a derivation of the Chinook Indian word "memalust," meaning "to die."

Facts: Established 2006 • 16 on-site acres • Also sources from Columbia Valley AVAs • 1,200 cases

Owner: Rob McCormick
Winemaker: Brian McCormick

Date visited: _____
Went with: _____
Notes: _____
_____

view

anciness

ck/patio

d for sale

cnic area

bus/rv

t friendly

tours

ent space

Mt. Hood Winery

www.mthoodwinery.com
1930 Hwy 35; Hood River; 541.386.8333

Hours: Daily 11:00am–5:00pm (mid-April–Nov)

Tasting Fee: $5.00 for 6+ tastes

Wine: 8 varieties; $12.00-$28.00
Specializes in 100% estate Pinot Noir and Pinot Gris

Outside: Wow! The views here are amazing! There are few other places where you can see Mt. Adams *and* Mt. Hood so clearly and seemingly close up. Although new, they've gone all out with landscaping as well. The building itself is a stunner with quality NW style.

Inside: Giant windows, soaring ceilings to continue the majestic effect and attention to detail throughout.

Notes: Winery and other vineyard not located on property. • This has to be one of the best places in the world to get married. Fall in love and book it soon! • Be advised to prepare for crowds – this place has it all and is destined to become extremely popular.

Facts: Established 2002 • 35 acres • Columbia Valley AVA • 2,000 cases annually

Owners: Brothers Steve and Don Bickford
Winemaker: Rich Cushman

Date visited: _____
Went with: _____
Notes: _____
_____

view

fanciness

deck/patio

food for sale

picnic area

bus/rv

pet friendly

tours

event space

Pheasant Valley

• •

www.pheasantvalleywinery.com
3890 Acree Drive; Hood River; 1.866.357.WINE (9463)

Hours: Daily 11:00a.m-6:00pm (Apr–Oct);
Daily 11:00a.m-5:00pm (Oct–Mar); Closed Jan

Tasting Fee: $5.00 for 6 tastes;
$10.00 for up to 12 tastes with wine glass

Wine: 14 varieties; $14.00-$30.00
Specializes in Pear Wine, Pinot, Organics (no sulfites)

Outside: Spectacular view of Mt. Hood! Single lane
road takes you to the top of the world and perfection
in Pinots, picnicking and porch sitting. You won't want
to leave, so plan ahead—there's a B&B here!

Inside: Rich, but cozy decor with a huge, antique
cherrywood back bar, gold walls, and stone fireplace.

Notes: In a former life, the winery was a packing
plant for pears and apples. • Wild pheasants are
present at this perfectly pleasant place. • Gorgeous
inside and out for weddings, events and parties.

Facts: Established 2004 • 40 acres • Sources from
Columbia Gorge and Columbia Valley AVAs, and
crushes for others too • 5,000 cases annually

Owners: Scott and Gail Hagee
Winemakers: Garrit Stoltz and Peter Rosback

Date visited: _____
Went with: _____
Notes: _____

220

view

nciness

ck/patio

d for sale

cnic area

bus/rv

t friendly

tours

ent space

Phelps Creek

• •

www.phelpscreekvineyards.com
1850 Country Club Road; Hood River; 541.386.2607

Hours: 11:00a.m-5:00pm
(Daily Jul-Oct); Thurs-Mon (May-Jun);
Fri-Sun (Mar-Apr), Closed Nov–Feb

Tasting Fee: $5.00 for 6+ tastes

Wine: 12 varieties; $14.00-$27.00
Specializes in Pinot Noir and Chardonnay

Outside: Fore! The Hood River Golf Course clubhouse
is the unique setting for Phelps Creek's tasting room
right off the first tee. Bring your clubs and enjoy a
round at the historic golf course built in 1923.

Inside: Watch golfers drive and duff from your more
comfortable position inside the tasting room. There
are patio tables outside to enjoy in good weather.

Notes: The winery is named for Phelps Creek which
runs through the vineyard. • Summer BBQ weekends.

Facts: Established 2001 (first plantings 1990)
• 28 acres planted • Columbia Gorge AVA
• 3,000 cases annually

Owner: Bob Morus
Winemaker: Rich Cushman

Date visited: _____
Went with: _____
Notes: _____
_____

view

fanciness

deck/patio

food for sale

picnic area

bus/rv

pet friendly

tours

event space

Springhouse Cellar

www.springhousecellar.com
13 Railroad Avenue; Hood River; 541.308.0700

Hours: Fri–Sat 11:00am–5:00pm and Sun 1:00–5:00pm

Tasting Fee: FREE for 6+ tastes

Wine: 10 varieties; $15.00-$24.00
Specializes in wide variety of varietals and fun names

Notes: Old West, trading-post-style storefront in the Mt. Hood railroad station (head to that parking lot). Inside, it's a big, open, loft-like space with lots of character, giant wood beams and painted furniture. • Schedule a "field trip" and visit this downtown working winery. RSVP, and you'll get to see the "ruins" out back—cool area for a party or dinner! • Springhouse was named for an actual 1875 homestead springhouse on the owner's land which was their start-up storage and rumored turn-of-the-century wine cellar. • Request your flights of wine to be served up like microbrew samplers. • Refillable bottle system which is great for both the environment and your wallet (and 33% more wine, which is a much better size)!

Facts: Established 2004 • Sources grapes from local vineyards • Columbia Gorge AVA • 2,000 cases

Owners: James and Lisa Matthisen
Winemaker: James Matthisen

Date visited: _____

Went with: _____

Notes: _____

SYNCLINE

Syncline
• •

view

anciness

eck/patio

od for sale

cnic area

bus/rv

et friendly

tours

ent space

www.synclinewine.com
111 Balch Road; Lyle, WA; 509.365.4361

Hours: Thur-Sun 11:00am-6:00pm (Feb–Nov);
Sat-Sun 11:00am-6:00pm (Dec-Jan)

Tasting Fee: $5.00 for 3-4 tastes

Wine: 5 varieties; $16.00-$35.00
Specializes in Rhône varietals

Outside: The barn-style winery is surrounded by
a small grove of trees, an organic garden, and the
Celilo vineyard of Pinot Noir vines planted in 1972.
Take a hike up the hill for a look around the valley
and a view of Mt. Hood.

Inside: Old wine barrels find a new career as the
tasting bar in the production area of the winery.

Notes: The Bingen Syncline a.k.a "Coyote Wall Syncline"
was the inspiration for the wineries name. A syncline
is a geologic formation—a dramatic, towering trough
of stratified rock that looks like a sinking incline.

Facts: Established 1999; 36 acres (one acre planted
planted in Columbia Gorge AVA and sources grapes
from throughout Washington); 4,500 cases

Owners: James and Poppie Mantone
Winemaker: James Mantone

Date visited: _____
Went with: _____
Notes: _____

view

fanciness

deck/patio

food for sale

picnic area

bus/rv

pet friendly

tours

event space

Wheatridge
• •

www.wheatridgeinthenook.com
11102 Philippi Canyon Lane; Arlington; 541.454.2585

Hours: Daily 11:00am–6:00pm (year-round)

Tasting Fee: FREE for 6+ tastes

Wine: 9 varieties; $13.00–$25.00
Specializes in Syrah and lightly-oaked wines

Outside: You're in for an adventure of sorts, requiring a road trip "off the map" and a steep climb in your car, with roads flanked by giant drop-offs way up to the top of the "nook." Gorgeous amber waves of grain forever. Windmills and unique Oregon geography!

Inside: Very simple tasting room with very friendly service and a few gift items.

Notes: They win the best marked signage award, with signs to guide you every step of the five miles on the one road there is. • There's a "geo-cache" located here. • Family farm of 100+ years of wheat farming. Lots of history here with all kinds of stories if you ask!

Facts: Established 2004 • 2 on-site producing acres (sources grapes from throughout the Columbia Valley) • Columbia Gorge AVA • 800 cases

Owners: Larry and Laurie Bartlemay and family
Winemaker: Larry Bartlemay

Date visited: _____
Went with: _____
Notes: _____
_____

view

'anciness

eck/patio

od for sale

icnic area

bus/rv

et friendly

tours

ent space

Wind River Cellars

• •

www.windrivercellars.com
196 Spring Creek Road; Husum, WA; 509.493.2324

Hours: Daily 10:00am-6:00pm year round
(closed mid-Dec thru 1st week of Jan)

Tasting Fee: $10.00 for 6+ tastes

Wine: 12 varieties; $15.00-$30.00
Specializes in Tempranillo, Cab Franc and Port

Outside: Off the beaten track, but *wow!* Worth it!
The journey itself is quite a joyride with a long and
windy forest-lined road. Up top, enjoy the big deck,
light breezes and a spectacular view of Mt. Hood.

Inside: The tasting bar has the kind of view we all
want from our offices. Casual space with friendly
and knowledgeable staff. And they have crayons!

Notes: Check out "White Water and Wine" at
www.riverdrifters.net for a rafting and catered lunch
outing at Wind River Cellars.

Facts: Established 1997 • 20 acres (12 planted)
Also sources grapes from Horse Heaven Hills and
Columbia Gorge AVAs • 3,000 cases

Owners: Joel and Kris Goodwillie
Winemaker: Joel Goodwillie

Date visited: _____
Went with: _____
Notes: _____
_____

view

fanciness

deck/patio

food for sale

picnic area

bus/rv

pet friendly

tours

event space

Wy`East Vineyards

www.wyeastvineyards.com
3189 Hwy 35; Hood River; 541.386.1277

Hours: Daily 11:00am-5:00pm (Apr–Nov);
Sat–Sun 12:00pm–5:00pm (mid-Feb to mid-Apr)

Tasting Fee: $5.00 for 6 tastes

Wine: 5 varieties; $16.00-$28.00
Specializes in Pinot Noir and Pinot Gris

Outside: Driving up to Wy'East will remind you of an old fruit stand you would find along any highway in America fifty years ago. But their stellar garden decks are anything but ordinary. The view of their namesake, Mt. Hood, is blocked by their building. Picnic here!

Inside: The tasting bar is a long, antique buffet in a cozy room with brick-red walls, rustic wooden beams, ceiling fans and skylights, and a wee hint of Native American character.

Notes: • "Wy'east" is Native American for Mt. Hood.
• Around and about are views of three mountains.

Facts: Established 2005 • 20 acres Wy'East plus 8 acres Blue Chip Vineyard • Columbia Gorge AVA • 2,000 cases

Owners: Christie and Dick Reed
Winemaker: Peter Rosback

Date visited: _____
Went with: _____
Notes: _____
_____

Area Tasting Rooms

Bolton Cellars
www.boltoncellars.com
206 Court Street, The Dalles; 541.296.7139
Hours: Daily 3:00–close (opens at 2:00pm Sat–Sun summer);
Wed–Sun 4:00pm–7:00pm (off-season); closed on Tuesdays
Tasting Fee: FREE for 6+ tastes
Wine: 6-10 varieties; $14.00–$28.00
Two wine bars in one! The tasting room is located in a turn-of-the-century space with brick walls and wrought iron café chairs, or take a glass back to the surprise café in the flower shop next door. Live music Friday nights in the summer.

Jacob Williams
www.jacobwilliamswinery.com
421 State Street; Lyle, WA; 503.577.3906

Hours: Fri–Sun 12:00pm–5:00pm
Tasting Fee: FREE flight of 4 tastes;
Also a reserve flight $5.00 for 4 tastes
Wine: 8 varieties; $14.00–$30.00
Simple, welcoming, small house on main road in downtown Lyle, but plans to move out near Maryhill, with views of the Columbia River and Mt. Hood, by the spring of 2010.

Naked Winery
www.nakedwinery.com
102 2nd Street; Hood River; 800.666.9303

Hours: Sun-Thur 12:00pm-6:00pm; Fri-Sat 12:00pm-10:00pm
(weekend live music nights)
Tasting Fee: $5.00 flight of 6 tastes (or $1.00 per taste)
Wine: 17 varieties; $18.00–$34.00
Fun, big, colorful wine bar with naked art and great wine names with very creative writing on labels! Cascade Cliffs also hosts their wines in their tasting room on the river on the Washington side. Also has second label called "Oh!" (orgasmic) wines $35.00–$80.00.

Quenett Winery

www.quenett.com
111 Oak Street; Hood River; 541.386.2229
Hours: Daily 12:00pm-6:00pm (Fri–Sat until 8:00pm);
Winter hours Thur–Mon 12:00pm–6:00pm ('til 7:00 Fri–Sat)
Tasting Fee: $5.00 flight of 6 tastes
Wine: 11 varieties; $17.00–$29.00
*Well-decorated and totally chill wine bar with comfy
couches and tables, chandeliers, ornate frames, etc.
Occasionally offers absolutely delicious cheeses!*

The Pines 1852

www.thepinesvineyard.com
202 State Street; Hood River; 541.993.8301
Hours: Thur–Sat 12:00pm–9:00pm; Mon, Wed and Sun
12:00pm–6:00pm
Tasting Fee: $5.00 for 6 tastes
Wine: 18-20 varieties; $16.00–$38.00
*Nice, upscale wine bar with hanging gallery art pieces.
Tours of vineyard available with 3-4 day advance notice.*

Viento

www.vientowines.com
1930 Hwy 35; Hood River; 541.386.3026
Wine: 10 varieties; $14.00–$25.00
*Tasting room/winery coming soon (watch website). Guest
appearances at Phelps Creek or Pheasant Valley Winery.*

Waving Tree

www.wavingtreewinery.com
123 Maryhill Hwy; Goldendale, WA; 509.773.6552
Hours: Daily 9:00am–5:00pm (summer)
Tasting Fee: FREE flight of 6+ tastes
Wine: 12 varieties; $12.00–$20.00
*Ranger-style log cabin at roadside next to riverside park.
Visitor center inside too. Set yourself up for camping!*

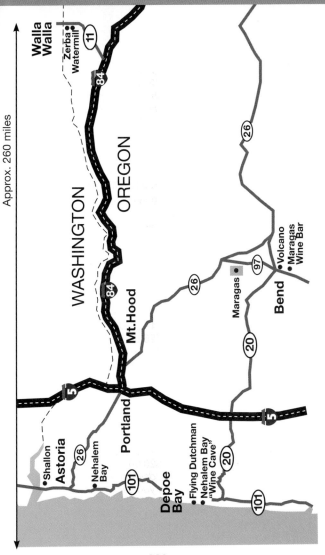

Approx. 260 miles

Walla Walla
• Zerba Watermill
(11)
(84)
WASHINGTON
OREGON
(26)
(84)
Mt. Hood
(26)
(97)
• Volcano
• Maragas Wine Bar
Maragas ■
(20)
Bend
(5)
Portland
Astoria
(26)
• Shallon
• Nehalem Bay
(101)
Depoe Bay
• Flying Dutchman
• Nehalem Bay "Wine Cave"
(20)
(5)
(101)

view

fanciness

deck/patio

food for sale

picnic area

bus/rv

pet friendly

tours

event space

Flying Dutchman
• •

www.dutchmanwinery.com
915 First Street; Otter Rock; 541.765.2553

Hours: Daily 11:00am-6:00pm (Jun-Sep);
Daily 11:00am–5:00pm (Oct-May)

Tasting Fee: FREE for a few tastes; .50 each for more

Wine: 15 varieties; $14.00-$34.00
Specializes in red wine

Outside: The spectacular ocean sights near the Flying
Dutchman will blow you out of the water! Head out
back to the party area and more ocean views.

Inside: All wood and appropriately nautical in tone
with a big, beckoning and irresistible gift shop.

Notes: Located near Depoe Bay, this the only working
winery right on the Oregon Coast. • Next to one of the
Mo's Restaurants (famous for clam chowder).

Facts: Established 1999 • Sources grapes from
throughout Oregon • 2,000 cases annually

Owner: Richard Cutler
Winemaker: Richard Cutler

Astoria Tasting Room
20 Basin Street; Astoria; 503.325.8110
Hours: Sun-Thur 4:00pm-8:00pm; Fri-Sat 'til 9:00pm

Date visited: _____
Went with: _____
Notes: _____
_____

view

fanciness

deck/patio

food for sale

picnic area

bus/rv

pet friendly

tours

event space

Nehalem Bay

• •

www.nehalembaywinery.com
34965 Highway 53, Nehalem; 503.368.9463

Hours: Daily 9:00am-6:00pm (year-round)

Tasting Fee: $5.00 for 6+ tastes

Wine: 15 varieties; $20.00-$35.00
Specializes in varietals and fruit-flavored wines

Outside: Not on the bay, but not far from the ocean.
On Hwy 53 one mile off Hwy 101. Picnic tables & deck.

Inside: Inside an old-German, cozy cottage with low
ceilings, dark woods and thick beams. Haunted?!

Notes: This place knows how to party! Both tasting
rooms are near the coast, they host outdoor concerts,
you can get married there, and you'll see their super
fun wine booths at events all over Oregon.

Facts: Established 1974 • Sources grapes from the
Willamette Valley and uses local fruit • 4,000 cases

Owner: Ray Shackelford
Winemaker: Ray Shackelford

Depoe Bay Tasting Room
22 S. Highway 101; Depoe Bay; 541.765.3311
Hours: Daily 9:00am-6:00pm (year-round)
Don't miss the very cool cave-o-wine!

Date visited: _____
Went with: _____
Notes: _____

SHALLON

decor

food for sale

event space

gift shop

Shallon Winery
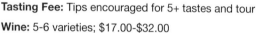

www.shallon.com
1598 Duane Street; Astoria; 503.325.5978

Hours: Daily 1:00pm-ish to 6:00pm (year-round)

Tasting Fee: Tips encouraged for 5+ tastes and tour

Wine: 5-6 varieties; $17.00-$32.00
Specializes in unique wines

Notes: This is a *very* unique place altogether, and you won't forget it! You'll get a tour, tastings and some history lessons, so you'll need to allow about 30-45 minutes. Slow down here! Relax. You'll learn something. • This will probably be the most pristine and museum-like working winery you will ever see. No view, but four "trope l'oeil" windows will tell stories that Paul will interpret. And you'll get a lot more stories if you can listen to him closely and fast enough. • Shallon was named for the winemaker's favorite local wild plant, Salal, or *Gaultheria shallon* (aka lemon-leaf), which makes excellent jam, jelly, or pie. • Paul does not use grapes to make wine. He uses other fruit, chocolate and whey! He is an inventor. • Located downtown with the entrance on 16th Street, up the stairs.

Facts: Established 1978 • 250 cases annually

Owner: Paul van der Veldt
WInemaker: Paul van der Veldt

Date visited: _____
Went with: _____
Notes: _____
_____

Watermill   **Zerba**

Walla-Walla in Oregon

While most of Walla-Walla wineries are on the Washington side, about half of the acreage of the AVA is on the Oregon side. In total, there are 70 wineries, 52 vineyards, 1,200 vineyard acres. Within Oregon: one winery, two tasting rooms, 750 vineyard acres and 31 vineyards.

Watermill Winery

www.watermillwinery.com
235 E. Broadway; Milton-Freewater; 541.938.5575
Hours: Mon–Sat 11:00am–4:00pm (year-round)
Tasting Fee: FREE for 6+ tastes
Wine: 12 varieties; $14.00-$24.00
The winery is located in the historic Watermill Building. Modern refurbished facility right in town. They also host Blue Mountain Cider Company. Summer nights on the patio with live music (Fri 5:00pm-9:00pm).

Zerba Cellars

www.zerbacellars.com
85530 Highway 11; Milton Freewater; 541.938.9463
Hours: Daily 12:00-5:00pm (year-round)
Tasting Fee: FREE for 6+ tastes
Wine: 45+ varieties; $16.00-$30.00 average (plus an array of a bit more expensive reserve or library wines)
Log cabin with style! All woody and new inside and out. Looks for the big "Z" on labels (look again – no zebras).

Maragas   **Volcano**

Central Oregon
• •

Maragas Winery
www.maragaswinery.com

Tasting Room at Winery
15523 SW Hwy 97; Culver; 541.546.5464

Hours: Tues-Sun 11:00am-5:00pm (year-round)
Tasting Fee: $5.00 for 4 tastes
Wine: 4 varieties; $14.00-$25.00
Large tasting room within winery facility. Outside patio with stellar views of pretty much every mountain in the area!

Tasting Room in Bend
643 NW Colorado; Bend; 541.330.0919

Hours: Sat-Sun 12:00pm-5:00pm (year-round)
Tasting Fee: $5.00 for 4 tastes
Wine: 4 varieties; $14.00-$25.00
Great outside courtyard patio near downtown Bend. And I must mention their fun, cartoonish labels!

Volcano
www.volcanovineyards.com
930 NW Brooks Street; Bend; 541.617.1102

Hours: Wed-Thur 2:00pm-8:00pm; Fri-Sat 12:00pm-8:00pm; Sun 12:00pm-5:00pm (summer)
Tasting Fee: $5.00 for 4 tastes plus sangria tastes
Wine: 4 varieties; $19.00-$29.00
Beautiful room with brick walls, cool tiles, artwork, a bar made of red wine barrels, and killer patio. Kid- and adult-friendly. Downtown with great nearby restaurants (next door to the Pine Tavern), but feel free to bring food.

Websites

Northern Oregon's Willamette Valley
www.willamettewines.com • www.oregonwinecountry.org

North Willamette Valley
Carlton area: www.yamhillcarltondistrict.com
Forest Grove: www.sip47.com
Chehalem Mountains: www.chehalemmountains.org

Central Willamette Valley
Dundee Hills: www.dundeehills.org
McMinnville: www.mcminnvilleava.org

South Willamette Valley
Salem/Corvallis Area: www.bentoncountywineries.com
Eugene area: www.wineriesoflanecounty.com

Southern Oregon
Umpqua, Rogue, Applegate, and Illinois Valleys
Applegate Valley: www.applegatewinetrail.com
Southern Oregon: www.sorwa.org
Umpqua Valley: www.umpquavalleywineries.org

Northern Oregon's Columbia Gorge
www.columbiagorgewine.com

Wine Country Guidebook
www.winecountryguidebook.com

Winery website links • Touring services • Events
Companion website to this book, website has direct links
to the wineries, events, transportation and accommodations
listings, and has many helpful tools to help you plan your
visit to Oregon Wine Country. Changes are added all the
time, so be sure to check in every once in a while. Sign
up for the monthly newsletter to stay in the know!

Other helpful sites:

oregonwine.org • winesnw.com • traveloregon.com

"Best-of" Lists

Memorable Views
Abacela
Anne Marie
Archery Summit
Bergstrom
Bethel Heights
Cowhown
Flying Dutchman
Lange
Lenné
Longsword
Maragus
Marks Ridge
Maryhill
Memaloose
Mt. Hood Winery
Noble Estate
Penner-Ash
Pheasant Valley
Redhawk
Sokol Blosser
Stoller
Sweet Cheeks
Trium
Van Duzer
Vista Hills
White Rose
Willakenzie Estate
Wind River
Wine Country Farms
Yamhill Valley
Youngberg Inn

Top Wedding Sites
Canas Feast
Cathedral Ridge
EdenVale
Elk Cove
Flying Dutchman
Laurel Ridge
Melrose
Mt. Hood Winery
Orchard Heights
Paschal Winery
Pfieffer

Schmidt Family Vineyards
Silvan Ridge
St. Innocents
Sweet Cheeks
Trisaetum
Valley View
Vista Hills
Wine Country Inn
Youngberg Inn

Gifts Galore
Chateau Bianca
Coelho
Duck Pond Cellars
Edgefield's
Eola Hills Wine Cellars
Evergreen
Flying Dutchman
Honeywood
Horse Radish
Kramer
Melrose
Orchard Heights
Plum Hill
RoxyAnn
Shafer
Tyrus Evan

Water's Edge
Airlie
Applegate
Aramenta
Julianna
Palotai
Paschal
Schmidt Family
St. Josef's

Sip & Stay B&Bs
Chateau Bianca
Delfino
Edgefield's
Pheasant Valley
Weisingers
Wine Country Farms
Youngberg Inn

Wine Favorites

Top 10 Lists

It's truly an impossible task to choose only ten favorites, but the following pages give you some carefully selected Top 10 Lists to reference for **favorite wines**, since throughout this whole book, I did not judge wines. I feel that overall, it is *so* subjective! Each vitner shines with pride over their creations. Every winery has something there worth visiting. Personal preferences vary widely.

To go in search of a great wine is an eternal quest that requires much research and following top writers in the field – and of course personal sampling! Taste preferences vary greatly from person to person, but if you recognize a few favorites on someone's list presented here, there's a good chance you'll agree on their other picks as well (and conversely, the opposite). These lists are a bit top-heavy on northern Oregon wines, as they are located closer to Portland, where all the contributors live.

To best discover your own personal favorites, be sure to attend as many wine tasting festivals as possible. Not only are they fun, they are the best way to taste and compare a wide array of wines back-to-back. Wine bars are good to check out as well, as most rotate their selections and host many of the Northwest's bests.

David Speer

Owner of Red Slate Wine Bar
107 SE Washington St. #133; Portland; 503.232.3876
www.redslatewine.com

Beran Vineyards – They only make about 700 cases of wine per year, but the wines are tasty. Bill and Sharon are fantastic people and are always a pleasure to visit.

Brickhouse – Doug has created an environment on his property that I haven't found anywhere else in Oregon. He is very focused on biodynamic farming and is a fantastic ambassador for this movement. His wines are great too.

Carlton Wine Maker's Studio – I love the variety of wine available here. This co-op has been the launch pad for so many great wineries, it's a great place to get to know the future stars of the Oregon wine community. The staff can be a bit cold.

Domaine Drouhin – They have fantastic wines, a great staff, amazing views, and an impressive facility.

J. Albin Winery – John makes the best sparkling wine in Oregon, and possibly in the US. His Pinot Noir and Pinot Gris are also top notch.

Lenné – This is a quintessential Oregon winery. Their Pinots are silky and approachable. The building is small and inviting. The winemaker/owner usually works the bar at the tasting room. Great little place with a few guest wines too.

Scott Paul – I think Scott's wines are very enjoyable. They're a bit lighter than some in Oregon. Scott also imports wine from Burgundy so you get to taste Burgundy next to Oregon.

Sineann Winery – Peter's wines are a great example of big wines with a lot of character and fruit. He sources fruit from all over OR, WA, and CA so you get to taste a range of wines and varietals.

St. Innocent – Consistently one of the best producers in Oregon. They keep their prices reasonable which is nice in the age of $50 Pinots. Their new facility outside of Salem is great.

Willakenzie Estate – Willakenzie makes big rich pinots that please almost everyone. Their staff is friendly and knowledgeable. The winery building and views are incredible.

Leah Jorgensen

Consultant / Wine Industry Marketing & Communications
www.leahjorgensen.com • 503.713.3277

Abacela Albarino – Crisp, refreshing, true to the varietal in every way – delicious!

Abacela Tembranillo Reserve – Full-bodied, balanced, smoky, complex, blackberry, raspberry, olive, plum, island vanilla – superb!

Argyle Extended Tirage Brut – quite possibly the best bubbly made in America – honeysuckle, white peach, ginger, beautiful.

Evesham Wood Blanc du Puits Sec – 85% Pinot Gris, 15% Gewurztraminer – lovely, elegant and great appertif for an al fresco dinner party.

J. Christopher Pinot Noir "Sandra Adele" – Silky, elegant, fresh flavors, a clean and sublime Oregon Pinot.

Marchesi Vineyards Cereja – A blend of Dolcetto, Sangiovese and Syrah, delicious, delivering light fruit and elegance.

McKinlay Pinot Noir Ladd Hill – There is a LOT of Pinot Noir in Oregon and it's becoming overly saturated, so I have become increasingly particular about the Pinots I drink. This guy is consistently amazing and I like that he's not trying too hard. Graceful wines, elegant Pinot Noir, as it should be.

Patton Valley Rosé – It's my favorite Oregon Rosé , dry with bright strawberry and rhubarb flavors, it's just pretty...

Remy Wines Lagrien – What a suprise, what a treat! She is my favorite up-and-coming winemaker. This wine is a delight, it's obscure and a bold move on her part. A native Italian varietal that is dark, big, bold, great structure – interesting!

Soter Vineyards Brut Rosé – A delightful bubbly—crisp, elegant and beautiful.

Leslie Palmer (with Gary Kneski)

Thirst Wine Bar & Bistro
0315 SW Montgomery Street, Portland; 503.295.2747
149 A Avenue, Lake Oswego; 503.697.1330
www.thirstbistro.com

Lange Pinot Noir 1997 – My absolute favorite wine I have had in my life! But any vintage of their Estate Pinot Noir is phenomenal!

Cancilla Cellars (any vintage) – Small producer of Pinots and a great Chardonnays a few years back. Excellent, extremely talented winemaker. Even the first garage blended wines are stellar!!

Sinnean Pinot Gris (08' Rocks!) You can't find earlier vintages – sells out! Never a bad wine…especially Pinot Gris. Perfect balance between acidity and fruit.

Thirst Wine Bar & Bistro's '06 Rose City Red – Created by Zerba Cellars – a true crowd pleaser!! Cab, Merlot, Cab Franc and more!

Oswego Hills Syrah (any vintage) – I tell everyone to pair this with popcorn. Phenomenal wine.

Four Graces Pinot Blanc (any vintage) – They get it right!

The Pines 1852 Zinfandel —Many excellent wines – '06 was harvested during a fire. So smoky! Been operating over a century in Columbia Valley. Never had a bad wine from them.

Anything from Shea Vineyard – Lots of different wineries source from this great vineyard. Deeply concentrated – supple, playful – palate pleasers.

Troon Vineyard A bit south, near Ashland – but worth the trip. Now has a tasting room in Carlton. Their Druid's Fluid is the best red blend made in Oregon that I have had, especially for that price point.

Elk Cove Ultima Riesling/Gewürztraminer/Pinot Gris Dessert Wine – supple. Like an ice wine. Best I've had in Oregon.
. . . .

Extra Credit – worth the fee. Archery Summit. The winery that caused us to fall in love with Pinot Noir!! Glorious!

Stephanie Hubbell

Three Degrees Waterfront Bar and Grill at Riverplace Hotel
1510 SW Harbor Way; Portland; 503.295.6166
www.threedegreesrestaurant.com

Adelsheim – One of the more well known wineries from the area. It's a great place for a history lesson.

Bergstrom – Always a favorite! For everyone, really. Their high-end chardonnays *never* disappoint.

Chehalem (especially the Three Vineyards Pinot Noir) – Their new tasting room is an added bonus. There are a lot of places you're going to spend an arm and leg to try one or two wines. They give you something ridiculous like 8 or 10 for about $5.

Cristom – Cristom's Viogier is smokin'!

Domaine Drouhin – Never fails to blow me away – both their wine and their tasting room. They have a way of making everyone feel welcome and special and are very informative without being condescending.

Elk Cove – Elk Cove's Rose is a crowd pleaser. But their Roosevelt Pinot....mmmmm.

Lange – Lange has one of my favorite views. Good place to enjoy a glass of their Freedom Hill Pinot.

Panther Creek – Always so underrated. Their wines are solid and whoever is in the tasting room is always very hospitable.

St. Innocent – Their Pinot Blanc is one of my tastiest treats of the moment.

Tyrus Evans – The tasting room is always a good time. Sometimes they even have a secret stash of Ken Wright stuff behind the counter.

Wine Friends Top 10 Lists

Del Profit's Favorites:

Anderson Family Chardonnay – Producers of great complex wines

Anderson Family Pinot Noir

Andrew Rich Malbec

Bethel Heights Temperance Hill Vineyard Pinot Noir – Old vines give it plenty of structure and earth.

Eola Hills Estate Pinot Noir – Only 12 bucks a bottle!

Montinore "Late Harvest Muller-Thurgau" – I call it white crack. Once you've had it, you cant stop drinking it!

J.K. Carrier "Provactor" Pinot Noir – Best value for a Pinot I have ever found.

Willakenzie "Kiana"

Willakenzie Pinot Blanc Great crisp white!

Witness Tree Estate Pinot

Helene Wren's Favorites:

Argyle • August Cellars • Cana's Feast • Cathedral Ridge • Four Graces • Ken Wright • Montinore • Penner-Ash • Torii Mor • Trisaetum

Sheri Coon's Favorites:

(Sheri is the Organizer of the www.meetup.com/ Oregon Wine Lovers Group. I totally agree with her picks!)

Apolloni • Boedecker • Canas Feast • Crater Lake Cellars • Gino Cuneo • Owen Roe • Pheasant Valley • Purple Cow • Roxy Ann • Seufert Winery • Silvan Ridge/Hinman • Sokol Blosser • Terra Vina • Tualatin Estate • Willamette Valley

Gordy Sato's Favorites:

Archery Summit • Erin Glen • King Estate • Marchesi Vineyards • Owen Roe • Ponzi • The Pines • Phelps Creek • Sineann • Viento

Wine Friends Top 10 Lists

Ed Querfeld's Favorites

Artisanal • Boedecker • Elk Cove • Ken Wright • Lange • Owen Roe • Panther Creek • Patricia Green • Territorial • Syncline (okay, technically Syncline is in Washington, but close enough)

Kurt and Sherrie L. Martel's Favorites:

(Wow! That's love to be able to come up with a list they can agree on! Okay, Steve and I are going to try that too. See below).

Andrew Rich Gewurztraminer Dessert Wine (e.g. Ice Wine)
Cathedral Ridge Halbtrocken – Great summer wine
Cuneo Syrah – WOW! (Now sold under the Cana's Feast brand)
Dominio IV Syrah – Absolutely THE BEST!!
Griffin Creek Cab Franc – A Willamette Valley Vineyards brand
King Estate Pinot Gris
Montinore Muller-Thurgau – Excellent value
Ponzi Chardonnay
Willamette Valley Vineyards "Hannah" Pinot Noir
Zerba Syrah

Cindy Anderson and Steve Woods' Favorites

(So yes, we cheated and picked more than ten! But we have tried almost all the wines in this book, so have a much wider group to manage than most. This is not a complete list, as none of the others are either. We stuck to places listed in this book.)

Adelsheim • Barking Frog • Bergstrom • Brandborg • Bryn Mawr • Folin • Hillcrest • Left Coast • Lenné • LaVelle • Seufert • Springhill • Stangeland • Syncline • Terra Vina • Territorial • Troon • Vidon • Viento • Willamette Valley • White Rose

Cindy also adds: Boedecker • Cowhorn • Domaine Serene • Erin Glenn • Marchesi • Montinore • Pfeiffer • Silvan Ridge/Hinman • Trium • Zenas • Zerba

Coupons

Find something you like? Stock up and save!

"You have only so many bottles in your life, never drink a bad one."

— Len Evans

Coupons can not be combined with any other offer. Not valid for further discounts off already discounted wine. Not applicable to Wine Club Member discounts. May not include library or reserve wines. Limits may apply.

Coupon usage rules are up to the individual winery. These coupons are being provided as a courtesy. Neither the author nor the publisher makes any warranty or representation about the validity or enforceability of the coupons.

Boedecker Cellars
15% off case of wine

Mixed wine styles or same.

St. Josef's Winery
2-for-1 concert admission

Limit one. Admission only (not good for wine or food).

David Hill Winery
20% off case of wine

Mixed wine styles or same.

Elk Cove Vineyards
10% off purchase of any wine

Individual bottles. Mixed or same.

Boedecker

www.boedeckercellars.com
2621 NW 30th Avenue; Portland
503.288.7752

St.Josef's

www.stjosefswinery.com
28836 S. Barlow Road; Canby
503.651.3190

David Hill

www.davidhillwinery.com
46350 NW David Hill Road; Forest Grove
503.992.8545

Elk Cove

www.elkcove.com
27751 NW Olson Road; Gaston
503.985.7760

WINE COUNTRY GUIDEBOOK COUPON

Montinore Estate
10% off purchase of any wine

Individual bottles. Mixed or same.

WINE COUNTRY GUIDEBOOK COUPON

Plum Hill Vineyards
10% off gift shop purchases

Excludes consignment items.

WINE COUNTRY GUIDEBOOK COUPON

Vidon Vineyard
10% off purchase of any wine

Individual bottles. Mixed or same.

WINE COUNTRY GUIDEBOOK COUPON

Laurel Ridge Winery
20% off gift store purchase

Discount on one item only. Gifts only. Wine not included.

Montinore

www.montinore.com
3663 SW Dilley Road; Forest Grove
503.359.5012

Plum Hill

www.plumhillwine.com
6505 SW Old Highway 47; Gaston
503.781.4966

Vidon

www.vidonvineyard.com
17425 NE Hillside Drive; Newberg
503.538.4092

Laurel Ridge

www.laurelridgewinery.com
13301 NE Kuehne Road; Carlton
503.852.7050

Horse Radish

www.thehorseradish.com
211 W. Main Street; Carlton
503.852.6656

Duck Pond

www.duckpondcellars.com
23145 Highway 99W; Dundee
503.538.3199

Sokol Blosser

www.sokolblosser.com
5000 Sokol Blosser Lane; Dundee
503.864.2282

Vista Hills

www.vistahillsvineyard.com
6475 Hilltop Lane; Dayton
503.864.3200

WINE COUNTRY GUIDEBOOK COUPON

Panther Creek
10% off purchases

Bottles of wine and/or merchandise.

WINE COUNTRY GUIDEBOOK COUPON

R. Stuart & Co. Wine Bar
Buy a bottle of wine, and get a free appetizer

Tasting room only. Limit one per table.

WINE COUNTRY GUIDEBOOK COUPON

Kathken Vineyard
2-for-1 summer concert ticket

Does not apply to all concerts. Call first for availability.

WINE COUNTRY GUIDEBOOK COUPON

Eola Hills Wine Cellars
15% off purchase

Minimum purchase $20.00. Does not include wine.

Panther Creek

www.panthercreekcellars.com
455 NE Irvine; McMinnville
503.472.8080

R. Stuart & Co.

www.rstuartandco.com
528 NE Third Street; McMinnville
503.472.4477

Kathken

www.kathkenvineyards.com
5739 Orchard Heights Road; Salem
503.316.3911

Eola Hills

www.eolahillswinery.com
501 South Pacific Hwy 99; Rickreall
503.623.2405

Namasté
15% off purchase of any wine

Individual bottles. Mixed or same.

Orchard Heights
25% off gift shop purchase

Gifts only. Does not include wine.

Van Duzer
Save $10.00! No tasting fee*

* When you buy one bottle of wine. (Fee applied to wine purchase).

Please note:

Many places, like Van Duzer as listed above, will refund
your tasting fee upon purchase of one or more bottles.
Exact policies vary depending on the winery, but always
inquire about how to get your tasting fee waived!

Namasté

www.namastevineyards.com
5600 Van Well Road; Dallas
503.623.4150

Orchard Heights

www.orchardheightswinery.com
6057 Orchard Heights Winery; Salem
503.391.7308

Van Duzer

www.vanduzer.com
11075 Smithfield Road; Dallas
800.884.1927

Please note:

Many places, like Van Duzer as listed above, will refund your
tasting fee upon purchase of one or more bottles.
Exact policies vary depending on the winery, but always inquire
about how to get your tasting fee waived!

Marks Ridge
20% off wine

Individual bottles. Mixed or same.

Springhill Cellars
20%-25% off wine

20% off individual bottles or 25% off full case (okay to mix).

Territorial
15% off case of wine

Individual bottles. Mixed or same.

Brandborg Winery
20% off wine

Individual bottles or case (okay to mix).

Marks Ridge

www.marksridge.com
29255 Berlin Road; Sweet Home
541.367.3292

Springhill Cellars

www.springhillcellars.com
2920 NW Scenic View Drive; Albany
541.928.1009

Territorial Wine Co.

www.territorialvineyards.com
907 West Third Avenue; Eugene
541.684.9463

Brandborg Winery

www.brandborgwine.com
345 First Street; Elkton
541.584.2870

Delfino

www.delfinovineyards.com
3829 Colonial Road; Roseburg
541.673.7575

Springhouse

www.springhousecellar.com
13 Railroad Avenue; Hood River
541.308.0700

Wheatridge

www.wheatridgeinthenook.com
11102 Philippi Canyon Lane; Arlington
541.454.2585

Wind River

www.windrivercellars.com
196 Spring Creek Road; Husum, WA
509.493.2324

VIP PDX – Wine Tours

www. vippdx.com
16869 SW 65th Ave; Lake Oswego, OR 97035
jennifer@vippdx.com • 503.348.3233

Eco-Wine Tours

www.eco-winetours.com
PO Box 230393; Tigard, OR 97281
info@eco-winetours.com • 503.863.7777

Martin's Gorge Tours

www.martinsgorgetours.com
PO Box 18177; Portland, OR 97218
Martin@MartinsGorgeTours.com • 877-290-TOUR (8687)

Vista Balloon Adventures

/www.vistaballoon.com
23324 SW Sherk Place; Sherwood, OR 97140
800.622.2309 • 503.625.7385
roger@vistaballoon.com

Index

Notes

....
....
....
....
....
....
....
....
....
....
....
....
....
....
....
....
....
....
....
....
....
....
....
....
....
....
....
....

www.winecountryguidebook.com